SCHOOLING YOUNG CHILDREN

SCHOOLING YOUNG CHILDREN

A Feminist Pedagogy for Liberatory Learning

Jeanne Brady

STATE UNIVERSITY OF NEW YORK PRESS

Published by
State University of New York Press, Albany

1995 State University of New York

All rights reserved

Printed in the United States of America

No part of this book may be used or reproduced in any manner whatsoever without written permission. No part of this book may be stored in a retrieval system or transmitted in any form or by any means including electronic, electrostatic, magnetic tape, mechanical, photocopying, recording, or otherwise without the prior permission in writing of the publisher.

For information, address State University of New York Press,
State University Plaza, Albany, NY 12246

Production by Christine Lynch
Marketing by Fran Keneston

Library of Congress Cataloging-in-Publication Data

Brady, Jeanne
    Schooling young children : a feminist pedagogy for liberatory learning / by Jeanne Brady.
      p.   cm.
    Includes bibliographical references and index.
    ISBN 0-7914-2501-0 (alk. paper). — ISBN 0-7914-2502-9 (pbk. : alk. paper)
    1. Feminism and education. 2. Critical pedagogy.
3. Multicultural education. I. Title.
LC197.B73 1995
370.19'345—dc20   94-28901
                                                                                       CIP

10 9 8 7 6 5 4 3 2 1

For Jack, Brett, and Chris

CONTENTS

Foreword by Paulo Freire		ix
Acknowledgments		xi
Introduction		1
Chapter 1	Critical Literacy as a Pedagogy of Empowerment	5
Chapter 2	Rethinking Literacy and Pedagogy	23
Chapter 3	The Politics of Difference	39
Chapter 4	A New Generation of American Schools	55
Chapter 5	A Feminist Pedagogy of Multiculturalism	83
Index		103

FOREWORD

It is with great satisfaction that I once again see and read proposals for the construction of schools that are democratic, where students are viewed as active contributors to their knowledge and not merely empty vessels in which teachers deposit an a priori chosen content to be passively consumed by students. Jeanne Brady's book *Schooling Young Children: A Feminist Pedagogy of Liberatory Learning* eloquently argues for the expansion of democratic spaces within schools where students are not viewed as mere consumers of knowledge who memorize pre-packaged information but as active producers of knowledge.

What is important in Jeanne's book is her insistence that educators should always resist the entrapment of falsely dichotomizing theory and practice. As she correctly argues, "separating theory from practice is one of the tricks used to reinforce the tendency to reduce professionals to people who merely enforce cultural policies far removed from the interests and needs of those to whom these policies are addressed." Her book *Schooling Young Children: A Feminist Pedagogy of Liberatory Learning* clearly demonstrates that what is not possible is to negate the practice for the sake of a theory that, in some fashion, ceases being theory to become pure verbalism or intellectualism. By the same token, to negate theory for the sake of practice is to run the risk of losing itself in the disconnectedness of practice. It is for this reason that I always advocate neither a theoretic elitism nor a practice ungrounded in theory. Like Jeanne Brady, I prefer to always work for a pedagogy that requires unity between theory and practice.

In her call for a feminist pedagogy of multiculturalism, Jeanne Brady emphasizes the need for intercultural dialogue that develops and maintains a linkage between the personal and the political. Her notion of an intercultural dialogue takes seriously the people's role in the process of becoming cultural beings. The process of becoming cultural beings involves not only reason but also affectivity. For a thorough understanding and respect for cultural differences, people's sensibilities should also play an important role. That is, we almost have to become quasi-cultural artists in order to fully grasp a deeper comprehension of cultural differences so as to also develop a deeper sensibility and respect for these differences. What we should always avoid is our often conditioned reaction to highlight cultural differences as a process to find inequalities in order to demonize and devalue the cultural "other." In other words, to measure cultural worth against a set of criteria derived from a blind acceptance of cultural chauvinism, a multiculturalist pedagogy that strives to be democratic must always adopt a position that embraces cultural difference not as an inferior/superior binarism. A democratic multiculturalist pedagogy along Jeanne Brady's proposal should view difference as a value when measured against the historicity and requirements of the cultural context that generates different cultural *modus vivendi*.

What becomes significantly clear in Jeanne Brady's book is that the real challenge is not to falsely celebrate cultural differences so to homogenize them. The real challenge is to find ways in which, as culturally different beings, we can strive to unify for the greater human principles of social justice, equality, and democracy. To that end, *Schooling Young Children: A Feminist Pedagogy of Liberatory Learning* is must reading for all those educators who believe that our young children can and should be viewed as cultural subjects who are agents of change.

Paulo Freire

ACKNOWLEDGMENTS

This book represents a journey in my professional academic life. It takes shape in two worlds, my world as an elementary school teacher for eight years and my role as a university professor. What I have done is take from these two worlds in an attempt to link theory and practice in a mutually informed way. Hopefully, this book represents a concrete example of this.

I wish to thank Estela Bensimon, Dan Marshall, Christine Jawork, Laurence Axtell, Jenny McLaren, Bill Tierney, Barry Weiss, Anghy Valdivia, Pat Shannon, Dorie Deegan, Martin O'Neill, Shirley Steinberg, Joe Kincheloe, Sarah Bomholt, Martha Angello, Roberta F. Hammett, Donaldo Macedo, and Peter McLaren. It is also with great appreciation that I thank my editors, Priscilla Ross and Christine Lynch, who have given me the space to complete this project. Finally, my three sons, Jack, Brett, and Chris need also to be acknowledged for grounding me in everyday life. Their energy and spirit continue to encourage and provide me with the desire to imagine a better future for them and all children.

INTRODUCTION

The world is undergoing a series of rapid cultural, political, and material transformations which position educators and others in a variety of new and shifting contexts. Across the globe, The New Right is launching a cultural offensive that presents one of the greatest challenges that feminists and other progressive forces have faced since the rise of Fascism in Europe in the 1930s. The cultural dimensions of the New World Order being created by the New Right stretches beyond national borders, transcends the traditional landscapes of the nation state, and reorders the relationship between time, space, and identity. The old divisions and boundaries which served to rigidly define subject disciplines, pedagogical practices, and the work of professionals are being crossed, rewritten, and reconstructed within a new international and global economy and terrain.

In what follows, I argue that multiculturalism and the issue of cultural difference has emerged as a primary force in shaping the conditions for public life at the current historical juncture. Changing patterns of immigration and demographics, increased numbers of single parent households, massive increases in children and adult poverty and homelessness all incorporate what I believe is the present day crisis in democracy.

Presently, the issue of multiculturalism is at the center of the debate about education and democracy. The conservative right-wing position has focused attention on what is alleged to be a crisis around the issues of authority, power, identity, and values in American society. What is being issued within the dominant language of the conservative position is an undemocratic approach to social authority and a movement to restabilize American life within the parameters of Eurocentrism, racism, and patriarchy. Much of this new cultural conservatism has attempted to reverse many of the gains made by women, gays and lesbians, ethnic and racial minorities, and other subordinate groups within the past twenty years.

Any analysis which is made from a particular standpoint is bound to be partial and unfinished, but the attempt to create an all-consuming universal discourse is incompatible with any liberating efforts. A feminist pedagogy of multiculturalism which produces a critical analysis of literacy and culture will progress by recognizing its own limits, engaging in a dialogue among different perspectives, and developing alliances based on the relevancies that different feminists and critical educators share.

A feminist pedagogy of multiculturalism that is critical and emancipatory will both challenge and break with unidirectional discourses which have made collective cultural production and criticism so difficult. Separating theory from practice is one of the tricks used to reinforce the tendency to reduce professionals to people who merely enforce cultural policies far removed from the interests and needs of those to whom these policies are addressed. Developing one's role as a feminist educator involves asking oneself questions about the nature of every theory and practice which determines the conditions of our environment. Theory as a form of both self and cultural criticism is concerned with the issue of who speaks, for whom, under what conditions, and for what purpose. Theory in this case is not innocent.

The following chapters are the fruit of my experiences as they have developed over the last fifteen years during which I have been an elementary school teacher, graduate student, parent, and university professor. These chapters are concerned as much with the development of my own attempts to ground my work in a theoretical discourse as they are with the pedagogical practices in which I have directly participated.

My book begins with an attempt to respond to the current crisis in democracy, literacy, and leadership. But rather than chart out the political and ideological cartography of this crisis, I begin in chapter one by articulating the fundamental categories that inform Freirean literacy and identify the major categories of Paulo Freire's work. Freire is central here not only because his work links literacy to a politics and theory of critical pedagogy, but also because it provides a tradition and referent upon which to extend and deepen the possibilities for what I call a feminist pedagogy of multiculturalism.

In chapter two I point to the strengths and weaknesses in Freire's work, by establishing the groundwork for connecting it with some of the insightful criticisms made by feminists and others of not only his work but also of existing modes of literacy and pedagogy. I am particularly concerned with the relationship between feminist theory and the politics and pedagogy of literacy. In this book I attempt to link the issue of literacy to the broader issue of creating the conditions necessary for the reconstruction of democratic public life. Literacy in this sense is informed by the broader project of educating students to advance the imperatives of a cultural democracy.

In chapter three I attempt to develop some basic elements of a feminist discourse of literacy by taking up the debate around questions of difference and identity. Essential to this chapter is the attempt to develop a rationale for making the politics of cultural difference and identity central to any viable notion of critical pedagogy and literacy. This suggests that a politics and pedagogy of difference not only offers students the opportunity for raising questions about how the categories of race, class, and gender are shaped within the margins and centers of power, it also provides them with a new way of reading history as a way of reclaiming power and identity. Moreover, a feminist pedagogy of multiculturalism provides students with the opportunity to acknowledge the relevance and importance of different literacies, narratives, and experiences as part of a broader attempt to critically negotiate and transform the world in which they live.

In chapter four I turn to an examination of *America 2000* and *Goals 2000* in order to both provide an exemplary model of the dominant discourse on educational reform and to employ elements of a critical theory and feminist cultural criticism in order to reveal its view of literacy as a discourse implicated in the construction of a particular form of citizenry.

In the final chapter I develop a feminist pedagogy of multiculturalism for elementary school teachers by contextualizing a connection between critical literacy, multiculturalism, feminist theory, and cultural democracy.

A feminist pedagogy of multiculturalism strives for education as the practice of freedom and moves toward a post-patriarchal discourse and social practice; that is, it is a radical philosophy of schooling aimed at restructuring the relations of power in a way that enables all children to speak and act as historical subjects within democratic social relations. Its basic premise is to end oppression while challenging the politics of domination in areas of not only gender, but race, class, and ethnicity. Gender, or any other form of difference, in isolation, gives us an important but disjointed and partial reading of a number of highly complex issues which coexist concurrently within cultural and economic realms. These categories of difference foreground forms of oppression and possibility that provide the basis for widening our understanding of how subjectivities, identities, and a sense of worth get constructed within and between various discourses and social relations as they are fought out at the level of everyday life. Difference and gender discourses provide not only new analyses for understanding how subject positions are constructed, they also reclaim the importance of linking the personal and the political as a legitimate foundation for how one speaks, what one says, and how one acts. In effect, these discourses have reclaimed the importance of difference and subjectivity as foundational to any radical theory of cultural politics, literacy, and schooling. Hopefully, these discourses will provide one of the crucial elements in the wider struggle over principles of equity, freedom, and justice.

1

Critical Literacy as a Pedagogy of Empowerment

Within the last decade, conservative and progressive theorists have placed the issue of multiculturalism at the core of the debate about education and democracy. Multiculturalism, to the conservatives, poses a problem. The conservative position sees contemporary America as a country that is in the state of moral decay. They perceive present day American life as being dismantled and Western culture being diminished by the concept of cultural difference that engages issues of race, class, gender, and ethnicity. Much of what depicts multiculturalism within the conservative position in schools is developed around a view of pluralism based on the notion of a "common culture."[1] A pluralistic view of multiculturalism recognizes that the "common culture" of the United States is made up by diverse racial and ethnic groups, yet it goes no further. Rather, its position defends the dominant culture and supports and contains those who are in power.[2] (Power, in this sense, means exercising control over others.) There is no attempt to interrogate the notion of power and how in some cases dominant groups are given more privilege while marginalized groups are silenced within this view of multiculturalism. Furthermore, there is no understanding how Eurocentric curriculum excludes and marginalizes the voices and subjectivities of children who do not exist within the confines of the dominant group.

To strive for a democratic multicultural society that challenges the totalizing and often racist views of a conservative notion of multiculturalism is a difficult task. But if we aspire to a goal of developing a critical citizenry whose actions are informed by democratic principles of justice that address issues of oppression and discrimination, then what is needed is a view of multiculturalism and literacy that provides a language for naming and transforming the ideological positions and social conditions that obstruct these possibilities. Hence, the concept of literacy is central to any notion of educational reform which presupposes a particular critical reading and transformation of the world. Literacy in this sense is informed by the broader project of educating students and teachers to advance the imperatives of a cultural democracy.[3] This project of liberation and social transformation will allow for the creation of multiple possibilities where hope is shared.

Within the dominant discourse, literacy is defined largely through liberal and conservative perspectives that tie its function to the dominant culture's ideological standards.[4] Basic skills and technical training permeate school curriculum in order to train students to become workers for jobs that require functional reading and writing. In this instance literacy is linked to the job market and serves specific economic interests.[5] In another form, literacy is defined by the need for understanding the masters in Western tradition which translates into a form of privileged cultural capital and serves to reproduce pathways to power.[6] In both instances literacy serves the dominant culture's ideological functions to sustain existing power relations.

For a multicultural democratic society to thrive, any discourse about literacy needs to acknowledge the multiplicity of literacies that surround us. In other words, it needs to address the question of social usage, which suggest at least three forms of literacy: functional, cultural, and critical. In this case, these forms of literacy would be linked to developing particular skills and knowledges that offer students a range of possibilities that would be necessary for realizing democratic public life. For example, beyond functional literacy, people need forms of literacy that provide multiple languages that allow communication across lines of cultural difference. They also need modes of critical literacy that challenge the idea of identity as singular, autonomous, and uniform; that is, a mode of critical and cultural literacy that provides three things. First, a critical literacy can provide the pedagogical conditions for understanding how identities are constructed through different subject positions. In other words, it allows students to see how they can and do make history in ways that think, feel, act, love, and create meaning to their world. Second, literacy as a critical and cultural discourse functions in this case as a form of address which provides the opportunities for understanding how subjectivities, experience, and power come to bear on educational discourse and practices. This enables students and teachers to understand how one's own subjectivity as well as others is constituted in language. Third, a critical and cultural literacy provides a location from which expression and action proceed. Put more sharply, literacy needs to be viewed within an ethical and emancipatory discourse that provides a language of hope and transformation that is able to analyze, challenge, and transform the ideological and social conditions that undermine it. In this case literacy is not a technical skill to be acquired or a "great book" to be read. Rather, literacy is a historical, theoretical, and ideological referent that allows for a pedagogy for understanding how people negotiate and translate their relationship to everyday life. Such a literacy would allow for a form of pedagogy which offers the relationship among discourse, social action, and historical memory. It is also a form of social praxis that is directed at self and social transformation which allows for the invention of new identities as active, social agents for social change. In other words, it offers an alternative form of literacy to the dominant discourse that gives a critical reading of how power, ideology and culture work to disempower groups of people while privileging others.

A pedagogy of critical literacy offers a language of critique that allows us to view major flaws in dominant educational theory. The use of the term pedagogy is deliberate, for it means much more than simply "teaching." Pedagogy is more complex and encompassing because it represents many aspects of educational practices that include the practice of a particular curriculum used within the classroom, the strategies and techniques used by the teacher, and how the curriculum is taken up by both the teacher and the students. This notion of pedagogy does not address methodology of classroom practices in the form of "what works" but rather situates practice within a realm of cultural politics. Therefore, literacy as a form of cultural politics allows us to explore the complexity of power relations as well as challenge the discourse of the dominant culture.

A critical literacy and pedagogy of empowerment are not new concepts but have evolved substantively over the past two decades.[7] Their roots can be found grounded in the work of Paulo Freire, the Brazilian educator and philosopher, who is viewed by many educators and social theorists as the most influential theorist in critical literacy and pedagogy based on his ability to interrelate theory, ideological commitment, and political practice.[8]

Before discussing the specifics of Freire's work, it is necessary to place Freire within an historical and a political context. Unless one understands the context of Freire's work, it is difficult to understand and interpret his pedagogy which is grounded in liberation theology and as a response to colonialist and imperialist settings.[9]

Paulo Freire re-articulated the politics of literacy in the early 1960s during the rise of a popular, radical revolutionary movement in Brazil. At that time the prevailing educational theory was dominated by positivistic and pragmatic assumptions. Freire's theory for education as a practice of freedom and liberation quickly became a popular alternative. His initial pedagogical formulations grew out of a concern for the masses of poor and uneducated Brazilian peasants exploited because of their illiteracy. Freire's liberatory pedagogy offered these people the necessary tools needed to struggle against their own oppression. Inserting literacy within a historical discourse, Freire argued that literacy was the precondition for not only forms of social and political agency but also social transformation and emancipation. In the most general sense, Freire's theoretical and political position generated an approach to literacy that addressed four major issues. First, it linked the issue of literacy to understanding how power, inequality, and domination undermine the possibilities for social agency. In doing so, Freire not only revealed how a sense of collective agency is fashioned within structures of domination, but how such structures can be understood and refashioned through a notion of literacy that is at once political and pedagogical. Second, Freire made it clear that literacy is not about simply reading the word, but most importantly about how people's social identities are constructed within asymmetrical relations of power. Literacy in this sense is not merely functional but is a productive force that signals how identities are shaped within an existing social order, become complicitous with that order, and also have the possibility of challenging existing relations of power. Third, Freire offered a theory of literacy that helped to illuminate how the dynamics of domination work at the discursive level. Refusing the essentialism and determinism that characterized many orthodox, left views of social change, Freire made the issue of literacy central to understanding the notion of cultural hegemony. After Freire, it becomes difficult to understand hegemony outside of the domain of language, pedagogy, and culture. Finally, Freire has not been content to simply retreat into the language of critique, to document how cultural domination works at the level of daily life; on the contrary, he has developed a notion of literacy that is propelled by a desire to create immediate and imaginary possibilities for redefining human agency and social struggle as both a political practice and a prospect for emancipatory struggle. Consequently, Freire developed a theory and practice of literacy within a discourse that appropriated many of the categories of critical social theory (these include existentialism, phenomenology, Hegelian dialectics, and historical materialism). Eventually, his proposal for a pedagogy for oppressed people had a major impact upon progressive educational settings, not only in Latin America but worldwide.

In what follows I will elaborate on the fundamental categories that inform a Freirean pedagogy of literacy and identify the major contributions of Freire's work.

TRADITIONAL EDUCATIONAL THEORY AS BANKING EDUCATION

Liberatory learning opposes conventional education in many ways. Traditional educational theory views knowledge as objective and in practice it incorporates a rote learning process described as the "banking model" of teaching.[10] In this model teachers possess objective knowledge and transmit this knowledge to waiting students who consume and in many cases are asked to spew it back without questioning the knowledge put forth. According to Freire this model of teaching turns students into receptacles to be filled by the teacher. The more completely he fills the receptacles, the better the teacher he is. The more meekly the receptacles permit themselves to be filled, the better students they are.[11]

Within this model, the teacher, on the one hand, is seen as the expert and holds authority over the important knowledge to be given out while, on the other hand, this model positions students in a way that requires them to take passive roles in order to succeed. "Banking education" reflects a particular view and set of values based on the attitudes and practices influenced by those in power. Freire lists the characteristics of this model:

(a) the teacher teaches and the students are taught;
(b) the teacher knows everything and the students know nothing;
(c) the teacher thinks and the students are thought about;
(d) the teacher talks and the students listen—meekly;
(e) the teacher disciplines and the students are disciplined;
(f) the teacher chooses and enforces his choice and the students comply;
(g) the teacher acts and the students have the illusion of acting through the action of the teacher;
(h) the teacher chooses the program content and the students adapt to it;
(i) the teacher confuses the authority of knowledge with his own professional authority, which he sets in opposition to the freedom of the students;
(j) the teacher is the Subject of the learning process, while the pupils are mere objects.[12]

In this instance, Freire speaks narrowly about methodology in a way that confirms the tendency of much of traditional educational theory towards microanalysis. Yet within this limited discourse around banking education Freire makes his central point: "the teacher confuses the authority of knowledge with his own professional authority, which he sets in opposition to the freedom of the student."[13]

In this model, knowledge is perceived as static and unchanging. There is no understanding of how knowledge gets produced or how knowledge needs to be extended to the voices and histories of the children in the classroom. Rather, inhabited in the unspoken experiences, students' own constructed knowledge, brought into the classroom resides hidden away in shame and worthlessness for some. Furthermore, issues that illuminate how class, race, sexual orientation, and gender function as part of the discourse of schooling are either ignored or subverted. Within the varied parameters of this discourse, there is a functionalism and reductionism that abstracts knowledge from power, equity from excellence, and ideology from cultural practices. Issues of management and procedure freeze knowledge and pedagogy in forms of monumentalism and transmission that deny the historically and socially constructed nature of all knowledge, discourse, and practice. Freire posits dominant educational theory less as an absence, an ignorance so to speak, than as a form of symbolic violence that is rooted in systematic forms of exclusion and marginalization. Rather than expanding on the notion of democracy, ethics, and social justice, banking education reflects the logic of the marketplace generated by the language of management, accountability, and efficiency as the primary platform from which students are taught to understand the world. In the final analysis, traditional educational theory is framed in a way that situates most students to conform, to follow authority, to accept a passive role imposed on them and to eventually become dominated by the institutional forces governed from above.

LITERACY AS CULTURAL POLITICS

Freire's compassion for human beings translates into a political commitment for equality, social justice, and empowerment. The basic foundation of Freire's theory is the project of liberation and social transformation. In other words, he believes that if our goals are shaped by the desire to live in a critical democracy, then it is necessary to construct new social formations that liberate and empower people oppressed by structures and ideologies which dominate them.[14]

Freire's pedagogy is multifaceted and incorporates two distinct yet integrated aspects of literacy: "reading the word and the world." In other words, emancipatory literacy requires us to read the text in the world dialectically.

> Reading does not consist merely of decoding the written word or language; rather, it is preceded by and intertwined with knowledge of the world.[15]

For Freire and Donaldo Macedo, understanding the world means understanding oppression in order to provide both oppressed groups and dominant groups with the possibility of acting upon and overcoming such oppression. In this case literacy is viewed as and in need of a definition in political and ethical terms. In effect, literacy cannot be disengaged from relations of power. By placing literacy within a realm of politics that views the social, cultural, political, and economic dimensions of everyday life as primary categories to be engaged, cultural workers, who in this case are educators, can understand how literacy functions to either empower or disempower people. As Freire and Macedo point out, "literacy is analyzed according to whether it serves to reproduce existing social formations or serves as a set of cultural practices that promotes democratic and emancipatory change."[16] Therefore, literacy as a form of cultural politics requires us to explore the complexity of power relations that both enable and silence social groups as well as challenge the exclusionary and often colonizing discourse of dominant culture. In practice, liberation becomes possible when the student can reflect upon the essentially constructed aspect of literacy production and in doing so is able to link a critical analysis of "words" with the "world." In addition, by discovering they are creators of culture, individuals also discover that they can transform culture as part of a broader struggle to eliminate diverse forms of oppression, while simultaneously inserting themselves as active agents and shapers of history.

CRITICAL PEDAGOGY AS LIBERATORY LEARNING

Freire views schools not as instructional sites designed only to transmit knowledge but rather as cultural sites that embody particular discursive formations and social practices that produce values, social relations, and forms of knowledge that legitimate the few who are in power. What Freire rightly challenges is the notion that schools convey a common culture, when in fact they support the dominant culture.

Although in saying this, I don't want to suggest that all cultural relations are asymmetrical in terms of power. Some relations are relations of equality. Nevertheless, according to Freire, all aspects of schooling are produced within cultural codes that produce and sustain particular forms of speaking, knowledge, cultural relationships, experiences, styles, and histories. In this sense, schooling produces a narrative in which selective histories, voices, and social identities fade in and out of focus, legitimated or marginalized on the basis of how particular forms of cultural capital sustain or challenge a dominant cultural agenda/hegemony. For Freire, literacy is the discursive face of power, domination, resistance, and agency. It both expresses the privileged positions of dominant groups in schools and it creates a referent for counter narratives and desires. Most importantly, literacy marks schooling as a cultural politics and site of struggle. Contrary to traditional educational theory, Freire's approach to critical pedagogy views knowledge as something to be analyzed and understood by students and informed by their own experiences and their understanding of the world. In this case, students become active participants in their own education by becoming "real" subjects in history. By learning to read the world critically, not only are students given the opportunity to break out of a culture of silence, but they are also invited to reclaim ownership over the process of change by taking control of the direction of their lives and histories. This is a pedagogy in which dialogue is the central category for recovering one's voice; it lays the foundation for emancipation.[17]

CRITICAL CONSCIOUSNESS AND CULTURAL ACTION

Central to understanding the world critically is the practice of "conscientization," the awakening of one's political and personal consciousness, which involves dialogue and critical analysis. In other words, critical consciousness becomes the crucial basis that exposes domination and creates knowledge about the distinctions between culture and nature. Within a critical pedagogy, the cultural experience of the students is the foundation for defining the social world, thus allowing for the opportunity to understand the concrete conditions of their daily lives, and the limits placed on them by oppressive situations. Such a pedagogy invites students to challenge these situations; therefore, the questioning of power and knowledge becomes the central element in the development of a critical consciousness through a problem solving process. Yet, conscientization is not an end in itself but is always joined by meaningful praxis (the dialectical interfacing of knowledge and power), which is generated by reflection and action. By emphasizing action/reflection in which the student views knowledge within her or his own concrete experience, rather than the rote learning process generated by the "banking model," the learner becomes actively involved as a subject of her or his own education rather than an object of the educational system.

Another critical element in Freirean thought is the rejection of vanguardism. He does not believe that intellectuals are the chief bearers of knowledge nor does he summon teachers to liberate people without their reflective participation which would objectify them. Rather, Freire stresses that both students and teachers be self-emancipated by taking charge of their own liberation. It is not the role of the educators to become the executors of transformation but rather, Freire defines a pedagogy of the oppressed as:

> a pedagogy which must be forged with, not for, the oppressed in the incessant struggle to regain humanity. This pedagogy makes oppression and its causes objects of reflection by the oppressed, and from that reflection will come necessary engagement in the struggle for their liberation. This is a theory of overcoming alienation, not domination.[18]

In other words, students and others must not share power simply over access to knowledge, but also over the conditions essential to the very construction of knowledge and culture. This is no small matter since it implies that people in any pedagogical site can only become agents when they are equipped with the knowledge necessary to make choices, shape their own identities, and insert themselves into the past and present as a fundamental part of their attempt to shape the future. Though it has become commonplace to identify Freire's pedagogy as politically charged, it is important to stress that central to his educational philosophy is the assumption that the act of knowing is never static but must be seen as meaning-in-process, which can only be understood through the lens of politics and power. Issues regarding who speaks, for whom, and under what conditions cannot be reduced or understood as merely methodological or empirical issues.

It appears (to me) that what is at stake for Freire is the issue of how power and knowledge come together within particular historical, social, and cultural configurations to produce specific cultural narratives, social identities, and ethical forms of address. For Freire, this is not only a hermeneutic or cultural issue. That is, he does not believe that every form of domination can be explained from or relegated to the spheres of culture and discourse. He is well aware that politics is, in part, about the effects of cultural practices, but that real pain, suffering, and domination exceed a merely cultural and discursive referent. The issue of the political has a social gravity that is about more than rationality and discourse; it has a material gravity that takes account of institutions, identities, and other material forms that cannot be only explained away through cultural and discursive analysis. The sphere of social and material gravity requires more than cultural analyses; it requires real action, struggle, and movement. Politics in the Freirean sense combines the theoretical importance of cultural critique with the grounding that action requires when it has to confront material forms of domination and struggle. Hence, critical pedagogy, as cultural action for liberation, is always driven by concrete political questions and concerns and while these concerns can be the focus of different struggles and interests, they need to address issues of inequality and transformation.

In pedagogical terms, Freire argues that fundamental to an emancipatory educational process is the communion of the nature of learning with the dreams, experiences, histories, and stories that students bring to their classroom. In addressing this connection, Freire writes:

> Narratives of liberation are always tied to people's stories, and what stories we choose to tell, and the way in which we decide to tell them form the provisional basis of what a critical pedagogy of the future might mean. Such a pedagogy recognizes that identity is always personal and social that while we cannot predict the path of

historical action or name human agency in advance, we can never give up the struggle for self-formation and self–definition such that domination and suffering in this society are always minimized.[19]

It is within these narratives and a language of critique that Freire requires educators to identify the nascent possibilities inherent in existing social relations. By linking critical knowledge with cultural action, people become active participants in society by shaping economic, social, cultural, and subjective formations that constitute their lives. Freire calls upon both teachers and students to participate.

> To invent new identities as active, cultural agents for social change means to refuse to allow our personal and collective narratives of identity to be depoliticized at the level of everyday life.[20]

By refusing to accept a static vision of the future in favor of one that speaks to a more liberated humanity, potentialities are created within a Freirean pedagogy for recognizing new social spaces, practices, and pedagogical possibilities.

LIBERATORY CLASSROOMS

In an attempt to test and measure knowledge, current reform movements reduce teachers to roles of clerks and managers, whose primary function is to service state documents and implement state mandates under the guise of accountability.[21] Furthermore, "teacher proof" curricula, typical of current educational management schemes is forced upon whole school districts to allow for "common" knowledge to be transmitted without error or deterrence. However, school curriculum needs to be defined in a way that doesn't view knowledge as static and complete merely to be transmitted from teacher to student. Rather, curriculum needs to be seen as a combination of not only knowledge but social relations and values that represent particular ways of life. What this means is that student experience, culture, and history must be given an important position in analyzing knowledge, always identifying it as a part of the relationship between culture and power. In this instance, teacher's roles are not seen as clerks but as transformative intellectuals who need to understand how school knowledge is produced, where it comes from and how it serves the interests of some while oppressing some. In addition, teachers must understand students' cultures within their classroom so as to confirm students' experiences, which are at times contradictory and need to be challenged, and to legitimate all students as subjects in history.

Freire's approach to learning offers both students and teachers the opportunity for empowerment. The liberatory classroom is an antiauthoritarian setting where teachers and students work and learn together. In Freire's terms, liberatory pedagogy requires a number of considerations. First, teacher/student relations must be viewed more dialectically. This suggests more than simply asserting that students must be actively involved in the learning process. It also suggests calling into question the ways in which power and authority structure the interrelated roles of teaching and learning.

For Freire, teachers and students must refuse to be either experts or simply learners. First, their roles must be mediated by the dual task of teaching and learning, producing information and critically mediating what is taught. This is not to suggest that teachers abandon all forms of authority or that their exercise of all authority is strictly authoritarian. On the contrary, Freire is insistent that teacher authority be asserted rather than abandoned within a project that provides the conditions for students to be able to learn how to exercise emancipatory forms of authority.[22] In this case, teachers have to become what Henry Giroux calls border crossers.[23] They have to learn how to listen to their students, be self-reflective about the nature and politics of their own location, and situate themselves in a form of ethical address that provides the opportunity for students to both speak and be responsible for the consequences of what they say without feeling terrified that their identities are on trial each time they venture into a new language or think and speak "risky" thoughts.[24]

Second, Freire politicizes the very notion of methodology by asserting the primacy of the problematic. That is, he believes that agency begins when students not only have access to different forms of knowledge, but also when they have the opportunity to interrogate all propositions, cultural practices, and disciplinary assumptions. To engage knowledge through dialogue is to assert both its historically and socially constructed nature, and its relationship to particular narratives and ways of life. Needless to say, for Freire, this is not a methodological assertion but a political and philosophical issue that makes dialogue and knowledge contingent upon cultural practices that advance rather than restrict the opportunity for students to name, read, and interpret the world critically as part of a broader project of recognizing the need to also change it when necessary.

Third, Freire is insistent that learning be related to the stories and experiences that constitute the narrative identities, in all of their complexity and contradictory nature, that students bring to school. In a more general sense, Freire is not just affirming student experience; he is making central to any form of critical pedagogy the issue of how such identities are shaped and produced outside of the immediacy of a given educational context. This suggests developing pedagogical processes committed to inserting students in forms of learning in which they become the subject rather than the object of knowledge, social relations, and forms of school organization.

Finally, Freire posits as part of his pedagogy the problem of how human beings learn. If subjects often become complicitous with their own domination, the issue of how they learn to insert themselves in beliefs and practices that contribute to their own domination must be understood as a pedagogical issue. Freire suggests that this is not merely an issue of rationality but also one of learning unconsciously through the gravity of social practices inscribed on how one learns through an infinite number of school routines, rituals, and relations.[25] In this instance, learning becomes an ongoing process in which a dialogue takes place around knowledge situated within the everyday lives and contradictory experiences of both the students and teachers who inhabit this space. Furthermore, based on a dialogic methodology, the problem solving process engages learners to see themselves as subjects in history by both understanding the limitations placed on them by the structures of domination and learning how to challenge and transform the situation. Therefore, to further enhance liberatory pedagogy, teachers must allow for the creation of new spaces to develop in their classrooms that allow different voices to be heard and legitimated in order to appreciate the nature of difference and develop a democratic tolerance for each other.

In the following chapter I want to build upon the work of a number of contemporary theorists to both critique and extend Freire's work, on the one hand, and theoretically expand the critical relationship between literacy and pedagogy on the other.

NOTES

1. The notion of 'common culture' erases the institutional, economic, and social structures that designate how dominant configurations of power privilege some cultures over others. See Diane Ravitch, "Diversity and Democracy: Multicultural Education in America," *American Educator* (Spring 1990), 16–20, 46–48.
2. Numerous sources on power and schools include Seth Kreisberg, *Transforming Power: Domination, Empowerment and Education* (Albany, N.Y.: Suny Press, 1992); Morse Peckham, *Explanation and Power* (Minneapolis, MN: University of Minnesota Press, 1979); Stuart Clegg, *Frameworks of Power* (Newbery Park,CA: Sage Publishers, 1989); Steven Likes, ed. *Power* (New York: NYU Press, 1986); Thomas Wartenberg, ed. *Rethinking Power* (Albany, N.Y.: Suny Press, 1992); Dennis Wrong, *Power* (Chicago: Univ. of Chicago Press, 1988).
3. For an analysis of the relationship between literacy, democracy, and critical citizenship, see Henry A. Giroux, *Schooling and the Struggle for Public Life* (Minneapolis,MN: University of Minnesota Press, 1988); Paulo Freire and Donaldo Macedo, *Literacy: Reading the Word and the World* (New York: Bergin and Garvey, 1987); Patrick Shannon, ed., *Becoming Political* (Portsmouth, N.H.: Heinemann, 1992); Colin Lankshear and Peter McLaren, eds., *Critical Literacy* (Albany, New York: SUNY Press, 1993).
4. For an excellent history and analysis of the literacy movement in North America, see John Willinsky, *The New Literacy* (New York: Routledge, 1990); Patrick Shannon, *Broken Promises* (New York: Bergin and Garvey, 1989). For an excellent analysis of the range of conservative and right wing views of literacy, see Candace Mitchell and Kathleen Weiler (eds.) *Rewriting Literacy: Culture and the Discourse of the Other* (New York: Bergin and Garvey, 1992). One of the most comprehensive analyses of lit-

eracy as a form of cultural politics can be found in William C. Green, *After the New English: Cultural Politics and English Curriculum Change,* Ph.D. Dissertation, Murdoch University, 1991; Allan Block, *Occupied Readings* (New York: Garland Publishing, 1995).

5. Roger I. Simon, Don Dippo, and Arleen Schenke, *Learning Work: A Critical Pedagogy of Work Education* (New York: Routledge, 1991).
6. Two most recent examples of this position can be found in Alan Bloom, *The Closing of the American Mind* (New York: Simon and Schuster, 1987); E. D. Hirsch, Jr. *Cultural Literacy: What Every American Needs to Know* (Boston: Houghton-Mifflin, 1987); Dinish D'Souza, *Illiberal Education* (New York: The Free Press, 1991).
7. See Patrick Shannon, *Broken Promises* (New York: Bergin and Garvey Press, 1989); Harvey Graff, *Literacy and Social Development in the West* (Cambridge: Cambridge University Press, 1981); Donaldo Macedo, *Literacies of Power: What Americans Aren't Allowed to Know* (Boulder, CO: Westview, 1994).
8. Paulo Freire, *Cultural Action for Freedom* (Cambridge: Harvard Educational Review, 1970); Paulo Freire, *Pedagogy of the Oppressed* (London: Penguin Books, 1972); Paulo Freire, *Education for Critical Consciousness* (New York: Seabury Press, 1973); Paulo Freire, *Pedagogy in Process* (New York: Seabury Press, 1978); Paulo Freire, *The Politics of Education* (New York: Bergin and Garvey Press, 1985); Paulo Freire and Donaldo Macedo, *Literacy: Reading the Word and the World* (New York: Bergin and Garvey, 1987); Paulo Freire and Ira Shor, *A Pedagogy for Liberation* (New York: Bergin and Garvey Press, 1987); Paulo Freire, *Pedagogy of Hope* (New York: Continuum, 1994).
9. See Carlos Torres, "From Pedagogy of Oppression to A Luta Continina," Peter McLaren and Peter Leonard, eds. *Paulo Freire: A Critical Encounter* (New York: Routledge, 1993).
10. For a representative collection of traditional, liberal, and radical discourses in curriculum theory, see Henry A. Giroux, Anthony N. Penna, and William F. Pinar, eds. *Curriculum and Instruction* (Berkeley: McCutchan Publishing Company, 1981); James R. Gress and David Purpel, eds. *Curriculum: An Introduction to the Field* (Berkeley: McCutchan Publishing Company, 1988); William Schubert, *Curriculum Perspective, Paradigm, and Possibility* (New York: Macmillan Press, 1986); David Pratt, *Curriculum Planning* (New York: Harcourt, 1994); William Pinar, *Understanding Curriculum* (New York: Peter Lang, 1995).
11. Paulo Freire, *Pedagogy of the Oppressed,* op. cit., p. 58.
12. Paulo Freire, Ibid., p. 59.
13. Paulo Freire, *Pedagogy of the Oppressed,* op. cit., p. 59.

14. Exemplary examples of this aspect of Freire's thought can be found in a number of chapters in Peter McLaren and Peter Leonard, eds. *Paulo Freire: A Critical Encounter* (New York: Routledge, 1993); Irene Ward, *Literacy, Ideology and Dialogue: Toward a Dialogic Pedagogy* (Albany: SUNY Press, 1994).
15. Paulo Freire and Donaldo Macedo, *Literacy*, op. cit., p. 29.
16. Paulo Freire and Donaldo Macedo, Ibid., p. viii.
17. A theoretical and practical application of this issue can be found in Bell Hooks, *Talking Back* (Boston: South End Press, 1989); Michelle Fine, *Framing Dropouts: Notes on the Politics of an Urban Public High School* (Albany: SUNY Press, 1991).
18. Paulo Freire, *Pedagogy of the Oppressed*, op. cit., p. 34.
19. Paulo Freire, "Foreword," Peter McLaren and Peter Leonard, eds. *Paulo Freire: A Critical Encounter* (New York: Routledge, 1993), pp. 6–7.
20. Paulo Freire, "Preface," Ibid., p. 7.
21. The most recent reform document that legitimates this approach is: *America 2000: an Education Strategy* (Washington, DC: United States Government Printing Office, 1991).
22. For two excellent discussions on the politics of authority from a feminist and critical pedagogy perspective, see Kathleen B. Jones, "The Trouble with Authority," *Difference: A Journal of Feminist Cultural Studies* 3(1) (1991), pp. 104–127; David Sholle, "Authority on the Left: Critical Pedagogy, Postmodernism, and Vital Strategies," *Cultural Studies* 6(2) (May 1992), pp. 271–289.
23. Henry A. Giroux, *Border Crossings: Cultural Workers and the Politics of Education* (New York: Routledge, 1992).
24. Roger I. Simon, *Teaching Against the Grain* (New York: Bergin and Garvey, 1992).
25. Peter McLaren, *Schooling as a Ritual Performance* (New York: Routledge, 1986; Philip Corrigan, *Human Capacities* (New York: Routledge (1990); Lois Weis, *Between Two Worlds* (New York: Routledge, 1985).

2

Rethinking Literacy and Pedagogy

In what follows I will explore present critiques of Freire, not in an attempt to reject or discredit his work but, rather, to extend and build upon what he has done in order to enrich and deepen its most emancipatory possibilities. More specifically, I want to examine some of the theoretical lacuna in Freire's work, especially in light of some of the theoretical gains that have been made by feminists and a number of other theorists in recent years.

Much of Freire's earlier work was developed within problematic elements of modernism. In his attempt to create a language of critique and possibility, Freire often has been constrained by binarisms and totalizing narratives that worked against its most valuable insights. One instance has been Freire's theoretical inability to name and address the often more extensive, multiple, and contradictory forms of domination and struggle that inhabited the larger social reality. Tied to an overemphasis on class struggle, Freire ignored the various forms of domination and social struggles being addressed by feminists, minorities, ecologists, and other social actors.

The most glaring example can be found in Freire's earlier work in which the subject and object of domination is framed in a patriarchal discourse.[1] Not only are women erased in Freire's language of domination and struggle, but there is no attempt to even acknowledge how experience is gendered differently. However, there is more at stake here than the refusal to treat identity and experience in gendered terms. There is also an unwillingness to address the complex, multiple and contradictory nature of human subjectivity. Consequently, Freire often falls into a theoretical discourse which legitimates a modernist notion of the unified human subject and its attendant emphasis on universal historical agents. A number of ideological trappings characteristic of modernism inhabit Freire's early work, particularly *Pedagogy of the Oppressed*, *Pedagogy in Process*, and *Education for Critical Consciousness*. In fact, underpinning Freire's emphasis on a totalizing narrative of domination, his support of a unified subject, and a universal historical agent, there is a creeping essentialism, one in which gendered differences seem frozen in a pseudo-universal language which subsumes experience and cultural practice within a patriarchal discourse. Before examining these issues in more detail, however, I want to comment specifically on how Freire's pedagogy has been taken up by educators in the West.

Freire is best known for his work with literacy programs in Brazil, Chile, and Guinea-Bissau. However, his work has gone far beyond its origins in Latin America and other Third World countries to be "reinvented" by educators and cultural workers in North America. In recent years, Freire's work has frequently been appropriated by academics, public school teachers, community organizers, and workers in adult education. Unfortunately, in a great many instances the political venture that informs Freire's work has been "forgotten" and what remains in these appropriations is a caricature of Freire's project. In the first instance, a number of Western educators have reduced Freire's politically charged pedagogy to an insipid and dreary list of methodologies dressed up in progressive labels that belie the truncated nature of the ideology that informs them. As McLaren notes,

> The critical theory to which Freire's work speaks must be extended in order to allow women as well as minorities to emerge as critical, social actors on the stage of human transformation and struggle. Furthermore, the conceptual frameworks that purport to uncover and transform the constructions of subjectivity need to be purged of their phallocentrism, Eurocentrism, and masculinist ideologies.[2]

Instead of situating Freire's work in a politics that provides the basis for transformative pedagogical practices, a number of Freirean based educators have largely displaced the political aspect of Freire's work for the safety of a list of prescriptive rules that allegedly add up to a model of critical pedagogy. While not unaware of the theoretical pitfalls that this approach produces, even well-versed Freireans such as Ira Shor appear to have fallen into this theoretical trap. For example, in a text designed to apply the Freirean approach to job training education, Shor promotes what he calls a nine point agenda for critical education. Situated within a topology that urges teachers to develop educational practices that are participatory, dialogic, situated, critical, and desocializing, Freire's work is denuded of the colonial context that informs it as well as the historically specific theoretical assumptions that give it meaning.[3] With few exceptions, the same approach to Freire's work can be found in the book, *Freire for the Classroom: A Source Book for Liberatory Teaching*.[4] In a revealing criticism of this book, Gail Stygall argues against the simple application of Freire's work to a North American context.[5] In her view, *Freire for the Classroom* is silent on a number of issues as a result of the depoliticization and decontextualization of Freire's work. According to Stygall,

> it fails to provide an analysis of the changes required in applying Freirean pedagogy in post-industrial societies; it avoids close scrutiny of the institutional sites of literacy training in this country, our schools; and with the exception of a handful of articles, the volume presents no adequate theory of language.[6]

At stake here is not simply the erasure of politics as part of a transformative politics, but the under-theorization of a critical discourse of literacy. Consequently, theory is subsumed within a reductionistic methodology and, while displaying the best of intentions, the appropriation of Freire's critical literacy by many North American theorists results in pedagogical applications that are often patronizing and theoretically naive. Simply to take a discourse developed by Freire for pre-literate peasants in Latin America and transpose the formative pedagogical assumptions that shape it to a population of students who belong to a highly industrial society, have been reared under the ideological banner of Western rationality, and are steeped in the legacy of colonialism without making problematic the politics of place, location, and translation that inform such a pedagogical process borders on imitating the very colonial logic that Freire was initially fighting when he launched his literacy campaign in Brazil. Pedagogical models based on recipe-like prescriptions of Freire's work, and applied from one educational setting to another are at odds with Freire's pedagogical and political project.

In short, what must be made a significant concern in taking up Freire's theory of literacy and critical pedagogy are the ways in which the process of negotiation and translation, when enacted in different cultural and historical settings, often contradicts the use of Freire's work as a revolutionary pedagogical practice, by sometimes trivializing the political project and in some cases eliminating it altogether. In what follows, I want to elucidate how some feminist and postcolonial theorists have begun to rewrite Freire's work in a manner less inclined to reify it as a methodology or romanticize it as a tradition that merely needs to be learned and applied. Recent work by theorists such as Kathleen Weiler,[7] Peter McLaren,[8] Henry A. Giroux,[9] and Abdul JanMohamed[10] has begun to engage both the strengths and limitations of Freire's work. In this context, the relation with Freire's work is "neither one of submission and repetition, but of transformation and critique."[11] In what follows I want to highlight some of the important insights produced by this work.

FEMINIST CRITIQUE OF FREIREAN THOUGHT

A feminist re-reading of Freire has argued against his exclusive focus on class as the only form of domination and called into question the abstract quality and limitations of certain terms—grounded in universal truths and assumptions—that narrow the collective experience of oppression. Feminists like Kathleen Weiler have argued that Freire's use of such terms as oppression, humanization, reason, and experience fails to engage both the multiple forms of oppression experienced by people of different groups and overlooks the political and pedagogical importance of addressing issues of identity and difference as they are structured through the contradictory practices of domination, struggle, and possibility within and between different groups of oppressed people.[12] Feminists have made clear that even though Freire recognizes the subject positions of the oppressed, he does not acknowledge the specific gendered realities of oppression and exploitation. This is evident not only in the gendered language that populates his early works such as *Pedagogy of the Oppressed*, but also his notion of reproduction as being exclusively linked to the project of economic reconstruction, especially in *Pedagogy in Process*. By focusing on reproduction around agriculture, Freire ignores the complexity of reproduction for women around the issue of women's work, i.e., health care, birthing, family matters. In effect, feminists such as Weiler and bell hooks have acknowledged that Freire's work needs to be supplemented by a theory of power that "restores a sense of 'both-and': a view of politics as fully dialectical."[13]

A feminist notion of difference reflects both diversity and unity and focuses on the lives of people who work and live in a multiracial, multicultural society. Again, Kathleen Weiler addresses the issues of difference as a central theme to expand on Freire's liberatory pedagogy. She points out the critiques of the essentialist position of a common women's experience based on the writings of lesbians, women of color, and postmodern feminists around the acknowledgment that no single women's experience can be conceived as universal. By identifying the possibility for multiple and sometimes contradictory positions, she illuminates how Freire fails to address "the overlapping and multiple forms of domination revealed in 'reading the world' of experience."[14] At issue here is the need for critical educators to reject the notion of identity as fixed or static, and to recognize and develop a project of multiple forms of liberation.

Indeed, a critical theory of literacy must come to understand how identities are constructed within multiple and often contradictory subject positions, how such identities shift, and how the struggle over identity takes place on many fronts, involving many different types of battles.[15] As Peter McLaren notes, Freire's theory of literacy and identity formation must be extended and deepened by acknowledging how the specificities of different historical and social conditions configure to produce within a changing matrix of agency and determination a range of diverse identities and subjectivities.[16] Educators must also engage the specificity of the subject positions of teachers, students, and others as they are defined by class, race, gender, and other subject producing forces. We must reject outright the notion that there is a universal subject and a set of common experiences that equally define all oppressed groups, along with those humanist discourses that enshrine "man" as the repository of human will and agency.

A number of feminists have also addressed the issue of authority and the role of the intellectual as developed in Freire's work. While few feminists, with the notable exception of bell hooks, have recognized that Freire does not equate all forms of authority with authoritarianism, feminists have nonetheless provided a critique of Freire's notion of authority that is as theoretically compelling as it is pedagogically useful.

Freire acknowledges that power is productive and not merely negative, and thus can be used to construct democratic forms of authority. He does not, however, consider adequately how the politics of teacher location inscribes educators within different degrees of strength or marginalization as a result of how they both describe themselves and are seen by others. It is not enough to respect the specificity of the voices that students bring to the classroom or any other educational site. It is also imperative to deconstruct the place from which teachers speak."[17] The places from which teachers speak always carry privileges for some and create hardships for others. These varied locations and the pedagogy of place they engender can be more fruitfully understood by analyzing how some feminist theorists have addressed the issue of teacher authority.

How authority is exercised by teachers is not an issue that can simply be generalized through an abstract discussion about the productive nature of power. Issues such as race, class, gender, and sexual orientation, as well as the particular material and ideological gravity of particular institutions, all affect how authority is both produced, sustained, received, and legitimated.[18] Weiler specifically reiterates this criticism from a feminist perspective and in doing so takes issue with Freire's overly abstract image of the teacher around questions of authority in relation to knowledge and power. Weiler notes that:

> Freire fails to address the various forms of power held by teachers depending on their race, gender and the historical and institutional settings in which they work.[19]

Weiler highlights the need for critical educators to address the concerns raised by a number of feminists around the central issues of difference, positionality and subjectivity. She is not content, however, merely to illuminate the discursive and ideological limits that structure the ways in which authority and power come together within the range of subject positions available to teachers. She also argues, correctly I believe, that any discourse on authority must address and transform the hierarchical structures of schooling that support a patriarchal society and ultimately serve to deny women authority.

> [T]he issue of institutional authority raises the contradictions of trying to achieve a democratic and collective ideal in a hierarchical institution, but it also raises the question of the meaning of authority for feminist teachers, whose right to speak or to hold power is itself under attack in a patriarchal (and racist, homophobic, class specific) society.[20]

It is thus necessary for feminist teachers to accept and exert authority, not in an attempt simply to gain and maintain power, but rather, in a positive way that also empowers both themselves and their students while simultaneously working to transform the conditions of institutional power. Weiler uses a feminist exploration of authority to advance Freire's position by providing a richer and more developed concern for authority that addresses the contradictions between the hierarchies of knowledge and power without denying the specificities of difference and the politics of identity.

> An acknowledgement of the realities of conflict and tensions based on contradictory political goals, as well as of the meaning of historically experienced oppression for both teachers and students,

leads to a pedagogy that respects difference not just as significant for students but for teachers as well.[21]

There are at least three important pedagogical concerns that are not addressed by Freire that need to be raised in the interest of deepening the possibilities of a critical pedagogy. First, teacher authority becomes emancipatory to the degree that it recognizes the importance of what I want to call a feminist pedagogy of place. That is, schools are by and large structured around ideologies, delivery systems, and goals that are largely competitive, hierarchical, and instrumental. Informed largely by a rationality that supports patriarchal practices, teachers' authority must recognize the important limits these forces place on producing knowledge, developing noncompetitive forms of learning, giving students access over the conditions necessary for the production of knowledge, and building classroom social relations that are democratic and just.

Second, authority in its emancipatory forms is never transparent or innocent. It is always a site of struggle involving issues of both access and definition. The issue of who speaks, for whom, under what conditions, and in what manner is intimately tied to a politics of representation that can only be understood by acknowledging how race, class, and gender shape power that legitimates certain forms of authority based on issues of exclusion and marginalization. Women and racial minorities need to represent *themselves.* This suggests that any discussion of authority must be rooted in identity politics that acknowledges the need for people to represent themselves within relations of power that dignify and support the specificity of their struggles, histories, and collective memories. This is not meant to romanticize experience, particularly the experiences of those who are oppressed. It is meant to suggest that such experiences must relate to having the authority to speak, and being held responsible for what one says and does in ideological and political terms. These issues have to be factored into any theoretical notion of democratic authority.

Weiler contributes to this analysis by identifying the notion of personal experience as a fundamental category in Freirean pedagogy that needs to be explored and expanded. She argues her position from a feminist perspective that emphasizes personal feelings and experience as a guide to knowing about the world. At the same time she addresses the limitations and contradictory moments of using feelings or emotions as a source of knowledge. According to Weiler,

> [t]here is a danger that the expression of strong emotion can be simply cathartic and can deflect the need for action to address the underlying causes of that emotion . . . shaped by the dominant discourses.[22]

Given this, she argues that feminist teachers need to understand how the authority of the dominant culture participates in the construction of emotions in shaping the identities of teachers, students, and others. Authority does not simply produce knowledge, but also plays a central role in constructing a pedagogy of affective investment, in producing and policing desires.[23] This does not suggest, however, that the sphere of the affective be linked to the forces of domination. On the contrary, Weiler and other feminists strongly argue that emotions and affective investments have an important role to play in shaping and understanding relations to ourselves, others, and the world around us. Moreover, the affective realm with its privileging of compassion, empathy, and solidarity reveals the limits of an exclusionary rationality that believes that meaning is only constructed through rational thought.[24]

Third, the notion of feminist authority must provide the conditions for students to become empowered within a pedagogy of place that allows them to speak without being terrified over the implications of what they say. The various discourses of feminism must work to create critical public spaces in which diverse discourses come into play, within an attempt to cultivate a critical spirit and form of ethical address that recognizes the importance of feminism as one of many discourses that can be used to promote human agency, collective struggle, and social justice.

THE POLITICS OF POSTCOLONIALISM AND POSTMODERNISM

A number of postcolonial theorists have aptly taken up Freire's work in a critical way. In doing so they address some of the major problems involved in appropriating and "reinventing" Freire's theories, transferring them to different cultural and historical settings. Central to such critiques is the recognition that many uses of Freire's work reveals an inadequate understanding of both the anticolonial project that informs his pedagogy and his dialectical theory of language. More specifically, lost in the translation of Freire's work is an understanding of his reliance on anticolonial and postcolonial discourses and how they radically structure his view of the relationship between theory and practice. In part, this means his work is often appropriated and recreated in ways that empty it of any understanding of the legacy of colonial struggle that informs it as a counter-narrative; at the same time, the sites of privilege and power in which Freire's work is used generally represent locations and sites of theorizing which are both complicitous with and unreflective about the legacy of imperialism. As Giroux points out,

> a politics of location works in the interest of privilege and power to cross cultural, political and textual borders so as to deny the specificity of the other and to reimpose the discourse and practice of colonial hegemony.[25]

Abdul JanMohamed has also commented on the risk that intellectuals from the First World run when they appropriate the work of Third World Intellectuals like Freire. According to JanMohamed, such intellectuals must be clear about "mapping the politic of their forays into other cultures."[26] Giroux attempts to take this position a step further by requiring educators to

> make problematic a politics of location situated in the privilege and power of the West and how engaging the question of the ideological weight of such a position constructs one's specific reading of Freire's work.[27]

This means that educators must negotiate and deconstruct the borders that define the politics and privilege of their own location. In developing this argument, Giroux calls upon cultural workers to become border crossers, as part of a self-conscious attempt to step outside the safety zone of the cultural, theoretical, and ideological confidence that informs both their work and structures their relationship with the oppressed "Other."[28] JanMohamed further reinforces this point by arguing that Freire's

> pedagogy implicitly advocates the nurturing of intellectuals who will cross borders and in the process develop strong antagonisms.... In so doing, they in effect become archaeologists of the site of their own social formation.... Their contemplation of the condition of their lives represents a freedom, or at least an attempt to achieve freedom, from the political of imaginary identification and opposition, from conflation of identity and location, and so on—in short, from the varied and powerful forms of suturing that are represented by and instrumental in the construction of their sedimented culture.[29]

By refusing to deconstruct their own politics of privilege and location, educators continue to maintain and produce forms of domination and oppression that are deeply rooted in the legacy of colonialism. As Giroux points out,

> From the comforting perspective of the colonial gaze, such theorists often appropriate Freire's work without engaging its historical specificity and ongoing political project. The gaze in this case becomes self-serving and self-referential, its principals shaped by technical and methodological considerations.[30]

Giroux further elaborates on the difficult task of using Freire's work. Not only does it change over time, it also carries with it a shifting political project. As cultural workers and border intellectuals we must constantly re-examine the sites and spaces in which we work as historical, social, and political borderlands which offer possibilities for refiguring knowledge, values, and identities so as to develop relations that can produce resistance to and relief from structures of domination and oppression. At stake here is the need for educators who use Freire's work to change the terms on which borders are both named and crossed. In his attempt to extend Freire's work from a postcolonialist perspective, McLaren argues that resistance to domination and oppression entails the development of a new language that avoids the binarisms of logocentric discourse.[31] Hence, there is a need to make clear what the terms of reference are that educators use to both speak from a particular place, to create the conditions for others to speak, and to reconfigure through specific pedagogical practices the relations between the centers and margins of power both within the school and between the school and the larger society.

Within varied postcolonial discourses, there is much concern over how Eurocentric practices displace the theoretical and political gravity of "third world" discourses as part of an effort to both appropriate (domesticate) them and to rewrite them as part of a Western hegemonic project. Postcolonial and feminist theorists have sought to rewrite the language of difference and culture outside of the monumentalist view of Eurocentrism. In doing so they have challenged the notion of authentic culture and humanist "man" as a unified, autonomous subject, while simultaneously emphasizing the role that cultural difference can play as part of a broader goal of creating diverse public cultures and further animating the conditions necessary for democratic life. In this case, Freire's original concern about making the issues of agency and identity central to the notion of difference have been expanded so as to increase the range of democratic antagonisms that underlie multiple forms of struggle and resistance.

Within this perspective, language does not become the passive vehicle of prescriptive methodologies. On the contrary, it becomes an active form of cultural production for "getting at" and understanding the things that shape our identity; it allows us to understand zones of cultural difference, and to create spaces where people can move beyond wooden topologies that lock them into rigid boundaries and identities. Moreover, in Freire's work, language becomes a referent for understanding how institutional practices privilege certain forms of identity, how one reads the world, and also how one refigures one's own identity within a specific set of historical, social, and economic configurations.

Finally, it is important to stress that Freire's approach to literacy, as it has developed over the last twenty years, represents, in the words of Cornel West, "a world-historical event for counter-hegemonic theorists and activists in search of new ways of linking social theory to narratives of human freedom."[32] His work has helped to rewrite the role of the committed and passionate intellectual who makes the concrete central to struggle without ever sacrificing the importance of theory and analysis. Although Freire's work has been subject to criticism, it is necessary to note that its richness, depth, and rigor have become a model for radical educators and cultural theorists all over the world. Freire's work is exemplary both in terms of its revelation of the man who produced it and the ethical address it constitutes through its call for democratic dialogue, collective empowerment, and social struggle. Freire's discourse has always been grounded in the noble utopian project of creating the conditions for human beings both to understand and make history as part of a broader project of constituting themselves as political subjects and ethical agents. Freire provides a legacy of dangerous memories that allow us to take up his work with love, care, and a sense of criticism that dignifies its own homage to resistance and engagement.

NOTES

1. This is particularly true of Freire's most famous book, *Pedagogy of the Oppressed*, op. cit. It is also important to point out that Freire has in numerous interviews and articles recognized the patriarchal ideology that was inscribed in his earlier work, and has both repudiated it and thanked feminists for bringing it to his attention. For a most recent example of Freire's views on this subject, see the excellent interview with Freire in Gary A. Olson, "History, Praxis, and Change: Paulo Freire and the Politics of Literacy," *Journal of Advanced Composition 12* (1) (Winter, 1992), pp. 1–14.
2. Peter McLaren, "Critical Literacy and Post-colonial Praxis: A Freirean Perspective," *College Literature* (in press), p. 10.
3. Ira Shor, *Working Hands and Critical Minds: A Paulo Freire Model for Job Training* (Chicago: Alternative Schools Network, 1988).
4. Ira Shor, ed. *Freire for the Classroom: A Sourcebook for Liberatory Teaching* (Portsmouth: Boynton/Cook: 1987).
5. Gail Stygall, "Teaching Freire in North America," *Journal of Teaching Writing 8* (1989), pp. 113–125; for a more extensive critique of Shor and his use of Freire's work, see Irene Gale, *Towards a Dialogic Pedagogy: an Interactive Model of Composition Instruction*, Ph.D Dissertation, University of South Florida, 1992.

6. Gail Stygall, "Teaching Freire in North America," op. cit., p. 114.
7. Kathleen Weiler, "Freire and a Feminist Pedagogy of Difference," *Harvard Educational Review 61*(4) (1991), pp. 449–474.
8. See the various essays by McLaren and others on Paulo Freire in Peter McLaren, ed. *Paulo Freire: A Critical Encounter* (New York: Routledge, 1993).
9. Henry A. Giroux, *Border Crossings* (New York: Routledge, 1992).
10. Abdul JanMohamed, "Some Implications of Paulo Freire's Border Pedagogy," *Cultural Studies* (forthcoming).
11. Strategies Collective, "Building a New Left: An Interview with Ernesto Laclau," *Strategies (1)* (Fall 1988), p. 12.
12. Kathleen Weiler, "Freire and a Feminist Pedagogy of Difference, " *Harvard Educational Review 61*(4) (November 1991), pp. 461–474.
13. Rosalind Brunt, "The Politics of Identity." In Stuart Hall and Martin Jacques, eds. *New Times: The Changing Face of Politics in the 1990s* (London: Verso Press, 1990), p. 157.
14. Kathleen Weiler, "Freire and a Feminist Pedagogy of Difference," op. cit., p. 469.
15. One of the best sources that engages the politics of identity and difference from the perspective of a number of political positions can be found in Jonathan Rutherford, ed. *Identity, Community, Culture, Difference* (London: Lawrence and Wishart, 1990).
16. Peter McLaren, "Critical Literacy and Post-colonial Praxis," *College Literature*, op. cit.
17. This issue is addressed in Linda Kintz, "On Performing Deconstruction: Postmodern Pedagogy," *Cultural Critique 16* (Fall 1990), pp. 87–107.
18. For a brilliant analysis of this issue from a feminist and critical theory perspective, see Kathleen Jones, "The Trouble With Authority," *Differences 3*(1) (1991), pp. 104–127; David Sholle, "Authority on the Left" Critical Pedagogy, Postmodernism and Vital Strategies," *Cultural Studies 6*(2) (May 1992), pp. 271–289.
19. Kathleen Weiler, "Freire and a Feminist Pedagogy of Difference," op. cit., p. 460.
20. Kathleen Weiler, Ibid., p. 461.
21. Kathleen Weiler, Ibid., p. 462.
22. Kathleen Weiler, Ibid., p. 463.
23. Peter McLaren, "Schooling and the Postmodern Body: Critical Pedagogy and the Politics of Enfleshment," *Journal of Education 170*(3) (1988), pp. 53–83.
24. For an excellent discussion of this issue, see Sharon Welch, *A Feminist Ethic of Risk* (Minneapolis: Fortress Press, 1990); Jane Flax, *Thinking*

Fragments: Psychoanalysis, Feminism, & Postmodernism in the Contemporary West (Berkeley: University of California Press, 1990).
25. Henry A. Giroux, "Paulo Freire and the Politics of Postcolonialism," *Journal of Advanced Composition 12*(1) (Winter 1992), pp. 15–25.
26. Abdul R. JanMohamed, "Worldliness-Without World, Homelessness-as-Home: Toward a Definition of the Border Intellectual," *Boundary 2* (in press), p. 3.
27. Henry A. Giroux, "Freire and Postcolonialism," op. cit., p. 16.
28. This position is especially developed in Henry A. Giroux, *Border Crossings: Cultural Workers and the Politics of Education* New York: Routledge, 1992).
29. Abdul JanMohamed, "Some Implications of Paulo Freire's Border Pedagogy," *Cultural Studies* (in press), pp. 14–15.
30. Henry A. Giroux, "Freire and Postcolonialism," op. cit., p. 21.
31. Peter McLaren, "Critical Literacy and Postcolonial Praxis," op. cit.
32. Cornel West, "Preface" in Peter McLaren and Peter Leonard, eds. *Paulo Freire: A Critical Encounter* (New York: Routledge, 1993), p. 1.

3

The Politics of Difference

In the previous chapter, I have argued that while proponents of critical literacy such as Freire and others have certainly extended the meaning of literacy to include not simply forms of knowledge but also their "meaning-effects," they have not paid sufficient attention to the struggle for liberation among and for diverse constituencies of women.

In this chapter I will attempt to develop in theoretical terms a feminist discourse of literacy and difference. In doing this I will take up the debate around questions of difference and identity informed by a feminist politics of literacy. Two main arguments will be developed as part of this project. First, I shall argue that in analyzing the relationship between identity and difference, literacy becomes a central term for extending questions about subjectivity, history, and experience. Second, I will develop the claim that a feminist politics of literacy provides the opportunity to take up these questions in an emancipatory way by translating them, not only into political issues, but pedagogical ones.

Over the last decade, feminist and critical theories of difference have greatly challenged mainstream perspectives on literacy. More specifically, a critical literacy influenced by feminist theory and poststructuralism has challenged traditional notions of language as reflective of reality and the self as a uniform, fixed, and fully autonomous agent of history. In this context, a dominant conception of literacy, with its emphasis on high culture, transmission pedagogy, and static identities, takes as its pedagogic goal the challenge of creating more literate students, versed in the dominant culture. In opposition to this view, feminist discourses in particular have attempted to develop a politics of difference in which pedagogy is rooted in the project of developing "students of literacy, who are interested in how various forms of written word dominate a culture."[1] In this sense, critical literacy situates knowledge and identity within a sphere of discourses, experience, and power as the latter are developed within a variety of multiple, cultural sites.

A feminist politics of difference adopts the position that language always acts rhetorically. Knowledge in this sense is never independent of the political and linguistic processes and purposes by which it is evoked.[2] Rather, language is viewed as the primary medium through which individuals socially construct their knowledge of the world. Language always provides particular understandings within specified communities of discourse. That is, meaning is always constructed within a space populated with discourses that mark, name, exclude, and inscribe. But language is about more than the intersection of meaning and difference. It also produces us as subjects, since discursive practices are what locate us in history (or at least our sense of history). Through language we name experience and act as a result of our particular interpretation of such experiences. The struggle over how to name and transform experience is one of the primary projects of a feminist/poststructuralist politics of difference.[3]

Recent advances in feminist theory have worked to rethink the politics of difference in a way that will expand the concept of power and agency in educational theory. In challenging the conservative notion of multiculturalism that keeps privilege and oppression alive as active constituting forces of daily life within the centers and margins of power, feminist and postcolonial critics have extended the debate on the cultural politics of difference so as to provide important theoretical insights into how such discourses either actively construct colonial relations or are implicated in their construction.[4] Post-colonial critics have made it clear that history and the politics of difference are often informed by a legacy of colonialism. What is constituted as accepted knowledge must be analyzed for the exclusions, repressions and privileges that often go unacknowledged in the language of educators and in the classrooms. The new politics of difference neither romanticizes nor idealizes marginalized people, as often occurs within pedagogies based on a liberal pluralism; on the contrary, its main emphasis is to forge new kinds of connections among ethnic groups, cultural communities and institutional and cultural practices.

Stuart Hall also takes up the notion of identity and difference in a way that further underscores the idea of the instability of identity—as something "formed at the unstable point where the 'unspeakable' stories of subjectivity meet the narratives of history, of a culture."[5] What Hall is suggesting is that identities cannot be fixed within closed systems of meaning. In other words, a critical reading of identity means that there exists no fixed or essentialist identities—only identities that are open to further inscription, articulation, and interpretation. The position taken here is that identities are never completed but always in the process of negotiation and translation.

For Hall and others the convergence of difference and identity is a marker not only for rethinking the self in multiple and contradictory terms, but also a dialogic process in which the issue of self-representation is constituted in our relationship with others. As Stuart Hall remarks:

> The critical thing about identity is that it is partly the relationship between you and the Other. Only when there is an Other can you know who you are.... And there is no identity... without the dialogic relationship to the Other. The Other is not outside, but also inside the Self, the identity. So identity is a process, identity is split. Identity is not a fixed point but an ambivalent point. Identity is also the relationship of the Other to oneself.[6]

In this case, the notions of identity and difference point to a rethinking of the meaning and politics of representation, while simultaneously seeking a fresh understanding of how to imagine a feminist literacy which does not fall prey to either essentializing notions of identity or overly-determined notions of the self, which freeze identity in the authoritarian gaze of a privileged gender and sexual orientation. Trinh T. Min-ha is instructive here in warning of the dangers that exist in conflating gender/identity/difference, however oppositionally conceived, in terms that reinforce the underlying structure of patriarchal binarism.

> Difference... is that which undermines the very idea of identity, deferring to infinity the layers whose totality forms "I." It subverts

the foundations of any affirmation or vindication of value, and cannot, thereby, ever bear in itself an absolute value. The difference (within) between difference itself and identity has so often been ignored, and the use of the two terms so readily confused, that in claiming a female/ethnic identity difference is commonly tantamount to reviving a kind of naive "male-tinted" romanticism. If feminism is set forth as a demystifying force, then it will have to question thoroughly the belief in its own identity.[7]

Cornel West best characterizes the distinctive features of the new politics of difference. First, he points out that the new politics of difference "gives up the monolithic and homogeneous for diversity, multiplicity and heterogeneity." Second, it "rejects the abstract, general and universal in light of the concrete, specific and particular." And third, the new politics of difference attempts to "historicize, contextualize and pluralize by highlighting the contingent, variable, shifting and changing."[8] West also points to the need to demystify the new cultural politics of difference by making clear its moral and political aims: to preserve the agency of marginalized groups, increase the scope of their freedom and expand the democratic principles that will create a better present and future.

Contemporary critics have also argued that individuals need to understand their ethnicity in terms of a politics of location, positionality, or enunciation. In order to say anything, one has to be positioned somewhere and the interrogation of this "place" is significant in understanding how one's identity is constructed through the play of history, politics, and culture. Stuart Hall argues that the discovery of one's positionality or location can be taken up around the politics of the new ethnicity. According to Hall, the concept of the new ethnicity means that individuals

> need to honor the hidden histories from which . . . [people] come. They need to understand the languages which they've been not taught to speak. They need to understand . . . the traditions and inheritances of cultural expression and creativity and in that sense, the past is not only a position from which to speak, but it is also an absolutely necessary resource in what one has to say. . . . So the relationship of the kind of ethnicity I'm talking about to the past is

not a simple, essentialist one—it is constructed . . . in history, it is constructed politically. It is part of a narrative. We tell ourselves the stories of the parts of our roots in order to come into contact, creatively, with it. So this new kind of ethnicity. . . . it is an act of cultural recovery.[9]

A large number of feminist theories have been developed over the past thirty years that have successfully unmasked racism in the contemporary feminist movement and in doing so have expanded on the notion of difference. The works of bell hooks, Trinh T. Minh-ha, Gayatri Spivak and others have situated women of color, Third World women and working class women in specific histories and in doing so have exposed how the racial and sexual imperialism embedded in American society attempts to either erase or rewrite histories (and identities) of the Other.[10] In other words, these critics have made clear how white, bourgeois notions of experience have been essentialized within the dominant strands of the feminist movement to speak for all women, regardless of their specific location in discourses of race, class, and sexual orientation. By situating their work within a discourse and politics of difference, feminists of color, in particular, have been able to enrich and redirect visions and joint struggles toward emancipatory possibilities that have often been ignored by the master narratives that guided much left oppositional work over the last fifty years.

Chandra Talpade Mohanty's work within feminist research also critiques the Eurocentric, racial and essentialist dimensions of contemporary feminist research.[11] Mohanty points to the tendency of some feminist theorists to reduce both racial and gender issues of difference into personal terms. The end result is the reduction of complex historical elements into binary oppositions which simply pits men against women. In this position, differences between the sexes are seen as the major focal point for domination. What is ignored are differences among diverse groups of women and differences that also acknowledge the importance of race and class. In addition, what Mohanty claims is missing from a large amount of feminist research is the recognition that women are not only marginalized within relations of domination, but can also be involved in establishing these same social relations. Therefore, Mohanty points to the need for a critique of the language of difference by not merely acknowledging difference, but rather, raising questions concerning the kind of difference that is acknowledged and engaged. For Mohanty, a postcolonial feminism must work at the level of political intersection around antiracist, antisexist and antiimperialist aims imbedded in a project that takes seriously the issues that collectively address difference, diversity, and power.

bell hooks is another feminist theorist who focuses on the politics of difference.[12] She attempts to rewrite the relationship between the margins and center of power by revealing how borderlands constructed through the intersection of race and gender invoke violence, bigotry, and exclusion. She calls for the need to both name the experience of different forms of oppression and argues that the naming of differences must also be linked to understanding how structures of domination function to place women of color within and not just outside feminist Eurocentric discourses. Deconstructing dominant ideologies, hook's argument provides a first step in understanding how knowledge both privileges and silences different groups under the ideological and discursive weight of racism and sexism.

hooks also theorizes the notion of "coming to voice." This suggests more than just recovering stories of the Other. hooks points to the need for all voices to be equally privileged so that educators and students can locate themselves in history in order to function as the subject of history rather than simply the object. Moreover, this insertion into history is not only about rewriting or recovering one's own identity, it is more fundamentally about recognizing how one's history is inextricably intertwined with other people's location in history.

In an attempt to explore discourses within feminism that offer alternatives to the language of control, I would like to combine a feminist discourse on literacy with the notion of difference that I have articulated in the preceding pages. By incorporating difference within the context of literacy, my aim is to provide an essential component for developing a broader notion of democratic struggle and social justice. Henry Giroux points to the emancipatory implications of what he calls a politics of difference:

> If a politics of difference is to be fashioned in emancipatory rather than oppressive practices, literacy must be rewritten in terms that articulate difference with the principles of equality, justice and freedom rather than with those interests supportive of hierarchies, oppression and exploitation. . . . This is a language in which one speaks WITH rather than FOR others.[13]

Peter McLaren takes up this point in a similar way.

> A critical literacy is, therefore, one in which the personal is always understood as social, and the social is always historicized to reveal how the subject has been produced in particular. Subjectivity is understood, therefore, as a field of relations forged within a grid of power and ethics, knowledge and power. It is worth emphasizing that a celebration of difference without investigating the ways in which differences become constituted in oppressive asymmetrical relations of power often betrays a simpleminded romanticism and exoticization of the "other."[14]

Yet, if we are to take seriously these emancipatory practices, then we must think of difference in relation to power. By exploring the complexity of the relations of power we are required to understand how relationships are produced between ourselves and others and how one's place is historically and socially constructed. Difference is embedded in cultural spheres that produce knowledge and identities. Hence, questions underlying how difference relates to the notion of power, history and self-identity must be raised. For example, what knowledge is revered? Whose histories are legitimated? Whose voices are silenced? What identities are marginalized or excluded within dominant discourses? How do we avoid romanticizing the histories of the oppressed? Mohanty's critique of a language of difference which refuses to take up issues of power and domination is worth quoting at length.

> Difference seen as benign variation (diversity), for instance, rather than as conflict, struggle, or threat of disruption, bypasses power as well as history to suggest a harmonious, empty pluralism. On the other hand, difference defined as asymmetrical and incommensurate cultural spheres situated within hierarchies of domination and

resistance cannot be accommodated within a discourse of harmony in diversity.[15]

Clearly the politics of difference and identity are more complicated than either humanist or radical essentialist discourses suggest. In order to move beyond these readings, feminists such as Mohanty, hooks, and Spivak have argued that educators and other cultural workers must consciously acknowledge and understand the barriers that exist between and among academic and nonacademic women, Third World women, white women, lesbians, and women of color; what is important to recognize here is that educators need to understand not only how relations of domination are produced, they must also work to transform the very ideological and institutional conditions that create them.

A DISCOURSE OF MULTIPLICITY

It is important to locate the concept of difference in a discourse that stresses multiplicity and views difference as a springboard for creative, political, and pedagogical change. The question of multiplicity is not only about acknowledging or registering difference. On the contrary, a critical feminist theory of multiplicity encourages a politics of difference that affirms women's experiences by allowing women to speak as historical subjects within diverse public spheres that offer them the opportunity both to engage various social issues and to transform public policy.[16] Furthermore, a feminist project of multiplicity attempts to provide a new way of reading the histories, identities, and knowledge of marginal people and in doing so offers a new way of refiguring and reclaiming power and identity. In effect, it is an attempt to shift and share power from the exclusionary and often colonizing discourse of the privileged to those groups in the margins and ultimately, by transforming the margins into multiple sites of power.

Critical feminist theories have rewritten the discourse of multiplicity in a number of important ways. First, they have made it clear that identity itself is constructed in ways that often accentuate the different, multilayered, and ever-changing subject positions available to diverse groups of women. Second, they have attempted to repudiate monumentalist discourses that legitimate all-inclusive explanations of domination, resistance, and struggle. In this case, they have accentuated not only how identity formation is rooted in multiple literacies but also how struggle is taken up in many forms based on the diverse forms of oppression under which women and others labor. Third, multiplicity has become a strategic referent for arguing against centralized forms of authority, and for developing mutually supportive centers of struggle. In this instance, there is no one literacy that can be used to both identify oneself or judge other voices as unworthy or inappropriate. On the contrary, when combined with a politics of difference and identity, the concept of multiplicity provides the theoretical basis for viewing voices differently—for hearing the unrepresentable, those "others" that illuminate new forms of ethical address and warrant new spaces for dialogue and forms of solidarity. Postcolonial theorist, Sneja Gunew, highlights some of the ideological and pedagogical implications of this issue:

> What remains is to explore other landscapes (or spatial representations) and literatures to rediscover the cultures and languages in which such concepts as the nomadic, displacement, identity of gender are figured differently. . . . We need to . . . think in terms of the mutual illuminations offered by juxtaposing various texts and reading for cultural difference in a non-binary manner.[17]

MULTIPLE LANGUAGES/MULTIPLE SPACES

There are many subject positions one occupies; each of us speaks from multiple places: student, teacher, race, mother, lover, friend, worker. As feminists we embrace a feminist concern about women, yet as academics we occupy different spaces of privilege (women of color do not occupy the same privileges as white women). In this sense, the issue of identity and location represents another avenue for addressing how differences get inscribed within different locations so as to extend or undermine particular social, political, and pedagogical possibilities. For example, being a feminist does not necessarily mean that one always escapes a complicitousness with maintaining and perpetuating the existing institutional structures in which one works. Being a feminist also does not guarantee that we will not perform pedagogical terrorism against students by closing down opportunities to challenge our views or to speak in a different voice. How might feminists speak in a way that invites people to listen? To dialogue?

In an attempt to speak and listen from a position of acceptance Gayatri Spivak calls for

> [the] unlearning of one's privilege, so that, not only does one become able to listen to that other constituency, but one learns to speak in such a way that one will be taken seriously by that other constituency.[18]

By engaging in the process of unlearning privilege, feminists can address and deepen the political and pedagogical aspects of a critical literacy in two ways. First, they must challenge the exclusionary and often colonizing discourse of dominant groups by carefully scrutinizing the legitimation of white middle class codes. On one level, this suggests becoming more self-critical and reflective regarding how identity and place come together around issues of power and domination. By attempting to shift paradigms rather than appropriate dominant languages and space, feminists can focus on developing strategies of communication and inclusion.

Second, by unlearning privilege feminists also need to confront differences constructively and successfully. Western women, of course, are not the only subjects in history; out of this recognition arises the political and moral imperative to understand and address the legitimate space that Third World women, working class women, and women of color occupy. Chandra Mohanty is correct in arguing for the "need for creating an analytical space for understanding Third World women as the subject of our various struggles in history."[19] Of course, this means more than being critical regarding how the Other is constructed, it also means coming to understand how feminists and others who occupy locations of privilege can come to unlearn their long-standing prejudices and misconceptions. For this to occur, educators and cultural workers must fight to transform those regimes of representation which inscribe both women of privilege and Third World women, working class women, and women of color in relations of domination and oppression.

Re-presenting Third World women and women of color as active subjects of history means decoding and challenging the traditional Western view of such women as passive, weak, and culturally homogeneous. In establishing this space and celebrating this position, feminist educators must not only reject essentializing representations which view Third World and women of color in reductive terms, they must also refuse to romanticize oppressed women. Most importantly, feminists must work to change both their conception of the Other as well as the reality that informs it. That is, feminists must work to create the discursive and nondiscursive conditions in which all women can act as subjects. This means recognizing those different zones of culture where identity and agency come together in historically and culturally specific ways. It means taking the specificity of the Other seriously. bell hooks takes this insight and offers some advice to marginalized women while at the same time indicting certain strands of white feminist theory.

> Third World women, African American women must work against speaking as "other," speaking to difference as if it is constructed in the white imagination.[20]

COLLECTIVE WORK

How then can a political community be reconceptualized within a feminist project? The political project situated in a feminist theory of literacies is the attempt to examine and restructure the way we view the relations of power that enables all women to speak and act as subjects within history. In addition, this project generates the possibility for shared literacies and dialogues that allow for multiple solidarities and political vocabularies. But for all of this to occur, it is necessary to situate this project in an arena of practice that initiates and encourages collective work. We should engage in collective and plural work for social transformation where diverse voices and discourses can be heard. This means, of course, acknowledging the different rhetorical situations and the different power relations that place women in dominant or oppressive positions.

It is worth noting that focusing on shared forms of oppression is neither unproblematic nor is it the only basis on which feminists can develop a politics of solidarity. In fact, bell hooks stresses that women should not celebrate their shared victimage as the essential commonality of women (since this reflects male supremacist thinking that to be female is to be a victim).[21] Instead, they should emphasize and organize around their sisterhood and their ability for self-determination. Extending hooks's point, I want to emphasize that a politics of solidarity should also include men who are in opposition to logocentric and hierarchical values within the hegemonic patriarchal system. This is not to suggest that women should not represent themselves as much as it is to argue that feminist politics is not limited to a specific gender. On the contrary, feminism represents a politics in which people actively participate in the shaping of theories and practices of liberation. In the particular case of feminism, bell hooks is instructive:

> I believe that women should think less in terms of feminism as an identity and more in terms of "advocating feminism"; to move from an emphasis on personal lifestyle issues toward creating political paradigms and radical models of social change that emphasize collective as well as individual change. For this reason I do not call myself a black feminist. Black women must continue to insist on our right to participate in shaping feminist theory and practice that addresses our racial concerns as well as our feminist issues.[22]

Solidarity and community work become the organizing principle for structuring relationships between self and others in order to analyze the interstructuring of sexism, racism, homophobia, and economic exploitation. Within these communities of accountability, marked by a shared commitment to developing democratic and emancipatory relationships among persons from diverse races and classes, new definitions of power and new patterns of relating across difference can be constructed. It is within these spaces that the opportunity can arise to explore differences in dialogue and in action as part of a broader attempt to gain insights into racial conflicts and to create empowering moments in the long and arduous struggle to transform society.

By organizing around a common concern, groups of persons from diverse racial, ethnic, and economic backgrounds can intersect and engage in dialogue that could provide opportunities for community participation, experimentation, and creative cultural production. Yet, where are these "communities of accountability"? Some already exist in local communities under such forms as community action groups, local religious groups, gay and lesbian organizations, university study groups, PTAs, to name a few.

CRITICAL FEMINIST LITERACIES

> In the same way feminists have learned
> to live with multiple meanings so should
> we be initiators of multiple literacies.[23]

A critical feminist literacy strives for a space that incorporates social practices of a politics of difference within a post-patriarchal discourse. More directly, it is an attempt to expose and challenge hierarchically ordered sexist and racist world views by restructuring the relations of power in a way that enables women to speak and act as historical subjects within democratic social relations. Its goal is to end sexist oppression and sexism while also challenging the politics of domination in areas of race, class, ethnicity, age, ableism, and sexual orientation. What a politics of difference provides is a more complex reading of gender that allows us to challenge other categories of difference. In other words, a critical analysis of gender serves to foreground multiple forms of oppression and possibility that provide the basis for widening our understanding of how subjectivities and identities are constructed within and between various discourses and social relations as they are fought out at the level of everyday life. What this means is that the critical interrogation of gender provides an essential element in the wider struggle over principles of equity, freedom, and justice. A politics of feminist literacies provides not only new analysis for understanding how subject positions for readers and spectators are constructed, it also reclaims the importance of linking the personal and the political as a legitimate foundation for how one speaks, what one says, and how one acts.

Without any attempt to change the concept of what constitutes literacy, society will continue to reproduce existing structures of power as well as continue to establish grounds for oppressive relationships.

Any attempt to change the cultural, political and social aspects of the dominant, patriarchal society will be seen as an attack on democracy. Yet, I am willing to take this risk because I believe that a feminist notion of literacy, one that initiates multiplicity, is fundamental as a discourse for developing a broader notion of democratic struggle and social justice.

NOTES

1. John Willinsky, "Postmodern Literacy: A Primer," *Interchange* 22(4) (1991), pp. 57–58.
2. There are many excellent feminist sources on this issue. Two representative positions can be found in Chris Weedon, *Feminist Practice & Poststructuralist Theory* (London: Blackwell, 1987); Teresa De Lauretis, *Technologies of Gender* (Bloomington: Indiana University Press, 1987); Diana Fuss, *Essentially Speaking: Feminism, Nature, & Difference* (New York: Routledge, 1989); Trinh T. Minh-ha, *Woman/Native/Other* (New York: Indiana University Press, 1989); Judith Butler, *Gender Trouble* (New York: 1990).
3. This issue is brilliantly explored in Linda Alcoff, "Cultural Feminism versus Post-Structuralism: The Identity Crisis in Feminist Theory," *Signs* 13(3) (Spring 1988), pp. 405–36. Also see Patti Lather, *Getting Smart* (New York: Routledge, 1991).
4. Representative examples of postcolonial discourse can be found in Edward Said, *Orientalism* (New York: Vintage Books, 1979); Rinajit Guha and Gayatri Chakravorty Spivak, eds. *Selected Subaltern Studies* (New York: Oxford University Press, 1988); Special Issue of *Inscriptions* on "Feminism and the Critique of Colonial Discourse" Nos. 3/4 (1988); James Clifford, *The Predicament of Culture* (Cambridge: Harvard University Press, 1988); Bill Ashcroft, Gareth Griffiths, and Helen Tiffin, eds., *The Empire Writes Back: Theory and Practice in Post-Colonial Literatures* (New York: Routledge, 1989); Howard Adams, *Prison of Grass: Canada From a Native Point of View* (Saskatoon: Fifth House Publishers,

1989); Homi K. Bhabha, ed., *Nation and Narration* (New York: Routledge, 1990); Gayatri Chakravorty Spivak, *The Post-Colonial Critic*, edited by Sarah Harasym (New York: Routledge, 1990); Ian Adam and Helen Tiffin, eds., *Past the Last Post: Theorizing Post-Colonialism and Post-Modernism* (Calgary, Canada: University of Calgary Press, 1990); Marianna Torgovnick, *Gone Primitive: Savage Intellects, Modern Lives* (Chicago: University of Chicago Press, 1990); Robert Young, *White Mythologies: Writing History and the West* (New York: Routledge, 1990); Gayatri Chakravorty Spivak, "Feminism in Decolonization," *Differences* 3(3) 1991, pp. 139–175; Benita Parry, "Problems in Current Theories of Colonial Discourse," *The Oxford Literary Review* Vol. 9 (1987), pp. 27–58; Abdul JanMohamed, *Manichean Aesthetics: The Politics of Literature in Colonial Africa* (Amherst: University of Massachusetts Press, 1983).

5. Stuart Hall, "Minimal Selves," *The Real Me: Post-Modernism and the Question of Identity* (London: ICA Documents, 1987), p. 44.
6. Stuart Hall, "Ethnicity: Identity and Difference," *Radical America*, 13(4) (June 1991), pp. 15–16.
7. Trinh T. Minh-ha, "Differences: A Special Third World Women Issue?" *Feminist Review* 25 (March, 1987), p. 10.
8. Cornel West, "The New Cultural Politics of Difference," *October 53* (Summer 1990), p. 93.
9. Stuart Hall, "Ethnicity: Identity and Difference," *Radical America* 23(4), pp. 18–19.
10. bell hooks, *Talking Back* (Boston: South End Press, 1989); bell hooks, *Yearnings* (Boston: South End Press, 1990); Chandra T. Mohanty, "On Race and Voice: Challenges for Liberal Education in the 1990s," *Cultural Critique 14* (Winter 1989–1990), pp. 179–208; Gayatri C. Spivak, "The Making of Americans, The Teaching of English, and the Future of Cultural Studies," *New Literary History* 21(1) (1990), pp. 781–798; Gayatri C. Spivak, *The Post-Colonial Critic*, Sarah Harasym, ed. (New York: Routledge, 1990).
11. See especially, Chandra T. Mohanty, "Under Wester" Eyes: Feminist Scholarship and Colonial Discourses, " *Boundary 2* 12(3) (Spring-Fall, 1984), pp. 333–358; Chandra T. Mohanty, "Cartographies of Struggle: Third World Women and the Politics of Feminism," in Chandra T. Mohanty, Ann Russo, and Lourdes Torres, *Third World Women and the Politics of Feminism* (Bloomington: University of Indiana Press, 1991), pp. 1–47.
12. See bell hooks, *Yearnings*, op. cit.; bell hooks, *Talking Back*, op. cit.
13. Henry A. Giroux, "Literacy, Pedagogy, and the Politics of Difference," *College Literature* 19(1) (February 1992), p. 3.

14. Peter McLaren, "Literacy Research and the Postmodern Turn," op. cit. p. 334.
15. Chandra Mohanty, "On Race and Voice," op. cit, p. 181.
16. Nancy Fraser, "Rethinking the Public Sphere: A Contribution to the Critique of Actually Existing Democracy," *Social Text 25/26* (1990), pp. 56–80. Also on the topic of difference, see William Tierney, *Building Communities of Difference* (Westport, CT: Bergin and Garvey, 1993)
17. Sneja Gunew, "PostModern Tensions," *Meanjin 1* (1990), pp. 28, 30.
18. Gayatri Spivak, *The Post-Colonial Critic*, op. cit., p. 42.
19. Chandra Mohanty, "On Race and Voice," op. cit., p. 180.
20. bell hooks, *Talking Back*, op. cit., p. 16; for an excellent analysis of this issue see, Chandra Mohanty, "Cartographies of Struggle: Third World Women and the Politics of Feminism," *Third World Women and the Politics of Feminism*, op, cit., pp. 1–50.
21. bell hooks, *Talking Back*, op. cit.
22. bell hooks, Ibid., p. 182.
23. D. Beckelman, "Defining a Feminist Literacy," *Canadian Women Studies/ Les Cahiers de la Femme 9*(3 & 4) (1988), p. 133.

4

A New Generation of American Schools

> These days questions of culture seem to touch a nerve because they quite quickly become anguished questions of identity. Academic debates about multicultural education similarly slip effortlessly into the animating ideological conflicts of this multicultural nation. How can the United States both respect diversity and find unity?[1]

In this chapter, I want to continue my analysis of literacy and its social role in the construction of the gendered, political subject. Specifically, I want to analyze how culture, identity, and difference are framed within a conservative notion of literacy and national identity. In what follows, I want to theoretically interrogate the underlying politics and ideology that structure the educational reform agenda of *America 2000*, and now, with some revisions, is identified as *Goals 2000: Educate America Act*. In doing so I want to offer a counter narrative to these documents, one which draws on many of the principles elucidated in the first three chapters.

As we move toward the twenty-first century the demographic character and ethnic composition of our nation is rapidly changing and shifting. The United States is becoming increasingly more culturally diverse and multiethnic. Within this context, questions concerning the relationship among identity, cultural difference, and democracy bear heavily on issues of national identity, particularly around the issue of education.

Not only do such changes make visible the fact that we are a nation of many literacies and cultural differences, but also call into question how educators and others will address the relationship between schooling and the reconstruction of democratic public life. I believe that the issue of education and cultural difference and its relationship to democratic public life presents one of the major challenges that educators must address at the present historical juncture. What is needed is a vision of the future that can help shape the present by providing a shared hope for liberty and equality. As our nation develops into a multicultural society, now, more than ever before, there is a need to develop a democratic public philosophy that respects the notion of difference as a central element of building a more just society.[2] What is needed is a language embedded in political intuitiveness that invites and encourages hope and possibility, a language informed by a discourse of justice, equality and democratic principles. Such a language must fundamentally oppose the current emphasis on hierarchical relationships, excessive individualism and bureaucratic rationality in favor of one that unites intellect and ethics with citizenship.

Admittedly, this task is a difficult one. But if educators and others believe schools are important public institutions that are vital sites for developing democracy, and if educators believe that education for citizenship and participatory democracy is an essential goal for educational reform, then they must address questions that bridge rather than rupture issues concerning cultural difference and social equality. Unfortunately, the Bush Administration set into action an educational reform movement that had a different set of objectives and this continues to hold true for *Goals 2000: Educate America Act*.

AN INEFFECTIVE EDUCATIONAL PROPOSAL

In early Spring, 1991, the Bush Administration released to the public *America 2000: An Educational Strategy*, an agenda which calls for the reordering of public education. This national educational strategy document was defined, in part, by two broad areas of concern. First, this reform package identified the areas viewed to be the most pressing roadblocks that hinder educational success in the United States. Second, it attempted to provide solutions to these problems.

America 2000 was organized more specifically around six primary goals and a number of strategies intended to help contribute to the educational process of every American individual. By the year 2000 this educational reform package hoped to achieve the following goals: every child will start school ready to learn; high school graduation rate will rise to 90%; each student in grades four, eight, and twelve will demonstrate competence in five core subject areas; American students will be first in the world in math and science achievements; every American adult will be a literate and responsible citizen and will have the necessary skills to live in a global economy; every American school will be liberated from drugs and violence so that schools encourage learning.[3]

In an attempt to meet these goals, *America 2000* offered a number of strategies. First, this document called for the creation of a New Generation of American Schools. These schools were required to meet new national standards in the five core subject areas of math, science, English, history, and geography. In addition, 535 New American Schools were to be devised as prime models with a target date for completion set for 1996. Each New American School would receive a large sum of money to begin operation, but would then be expected to succeed on a budget comparable to those of conventional schools.

These schools were to be developed by Research and Development Teams (R&D Teams). These teams were to operate in a partnership comprised of corporations, universities, think tanks, school innovators, management consultants and others, selected through a competitive process by the New American School Development Corporation, a private sector research and development fund worth at least $150 million. The R&D Teams were to receive up to $30 million each year over three years to invent these New American Schools.[4] Each school was to be located in an *America 2000* Community, designated by a team composed of the Secretary of Education, fifty-two state governors, and a panel of experts. Moreover, each community was expected to demonstrate a compliance with the *America 2000*'s four part challenge, which included: adopting the six national educational goals; creating a community wide plan to achieve these goals; developing a report card to measure progress; creating and supporting a New American School.[5]

Another component of the solutions offered by *America 2000* was "voluntary" national testing for students in grades four, eight, and twelve in the five subject areas. These tests were generated to help inform parents, teachers, politicians, and employers on how well national schools were doing. Special incentives for students in grade twelve who excel on these exams would be provided citations, intended to attract the attention of both colleges in their selection process and employers interested in people entering the workforce.

Choice was also mentioned as a strategy for positive change. The Bush Administration believed that parents have the right to choose the schools that they want their children to attend. The Bush Administration argued that this approach would increase educational standards by creating competition between public and private schools.

THE HIDDEN AGENDAS OF EDUCATIONAL REFORMS

America 2000 represents an attempt to exert powerful ideological influences on American schools and its nation's people. Approached from the perspective of a feminist politics of difference, what I see hidden within these documents is an attempt to offer a particular view and set of values designed as a vehicle for economic reform rather than educational reform. In effect, *America 2000* defines the purpose of American schooling by providing the American people with a discourse and form of ethical address that substitutes the language of democracy and citizenship with that of the marketplace. Appealing to the language of choice, competition, and self-interest, *America 2000* represents a full-fledged philosophy of school organization and culture modeled on the logic and principles of economic competitiveness. In this sense, these reform agendas are a "massive political experiment. It is not so much about education as about markets."[6] Hence, its objectives serve dominant American business and foreign policy interests while neglecting the most basic economic, social, and political demands of American schools.[7] Rather than expanding on the notion of democracy and social justice, these National Education Strategies pinpoint the logic of the marketplace, generated by the language of management, accountability and efficiency, as the primary platform from which public education must serve its democratic function. As Giroux and McLaren point out:

> *America 2000* can be understood as a wider ideological and political attempt by conservatives to divest government service agencies in favor of the private sector, redistribute wealth from the poor to the rich, and construct a privatized market system which enshrines individualism, self-help, management, and consumerism at the expense of those values which reflect the primacy of the ethical, social and civic in public life.[8]

I believe the hidden agenda within this reform plan needs to be exposed, especially within the context of three areas: reinventing new schools and communities, testing and standards, and school choice, and how these areas affect the role of teachers. Therefore, in what follows I will attempt to provide an analysis of the strengths and weaknesses of the recommendations offered by *America 2000* and, in addition, explore its omissions regarding issues of gender, race, and cultural diversity.

A NEW GENERATION OF AMERICAN SCHOOLS

A major component of *America 2000* is the establishment of a New Generation of American Schools in every community. According to the document, schools and communities will work very closely in an atmosphere of mutual support. R & D Teams will help communities in the development of their new schools, with plans for 535 new schools in operation by 1996. This strategy is flawed in many instances and marked by contradictions between outside experts and the emphasis on local initiatives. *America 2000* stresses the importance of individual school-based control, yet political intrusion by the White House has already occurred.

According to the document, the reform plan calls for R & D Teams to produce a new education system by disregarding "all traditional assumptions about schooling" and create "ideal" schools.[9] Rather than examine what programs are presently thriving, what this reform initiative does is undermine successful programs that currently exist. That is, rather than recovering and building on the important gains that have been made in existing educational reform movements, *America 2000* employs a bit of historical amnesia in order to displace any previous attempts to address the problems of American schools. Of course, there is more at stake here than historical amnesia, there is a politics of containment and erasure—one which refuses to engage the past in order to recycle the present as innovation. In addition, this proposal is so structured already with its requirement of core subjects and national standards that research and development will not have much room for innovation. Similarly, the call for active participation for teachers and parents will offer little more than the reproduction of educators already coerced into "teaching to the test" and parents who must sell raffle tickets to increase school revenue so as to pay for testing materials.

It seems illogical for a reform package to be put into play yet offer no commitment to federal funding of the program. As Deborah Meier aptly states, "I don't think there's any field other than education in which the President could announce a bold new plan for solving an age-old problem—and put no money behind it. 'We're going to do away with heart disease by the year 2000 and this is our plan: we're going to ask doctors to work harder and more imaginatively!'"[10]

America 2000 reform strategy for funding is through donations from business and the private sector. However, while it appears beneficial to involve the business sector of our communities, many questions arise. Corporate giants like AT&T, Xerox, and IBM who will invest large sums of money into these "new schools," will also want to take an active role in planning the curriculum and shaping the school. Is it not unrealistic to expect these corporate planners to "head the agency, design and award contracts, and put business figures firmly in control over educational research and development teams"?[11] Clearly, what is being articulated here is a notion of the citizen and subject that is both patriarchal and narrowly defined. A feminist perspective would elaborate on the issue of educating students to be leaders in the broad sense of being able to govern. Moreover, such a view would engage specifically feminist conceptions of the subject as multiple, contradictory, and gendered. Even the concept of work would be enlarged not simply to challenge existing capitalist assumptions about hierarchy and labor, but also to include questions concerning the role of women in the workplace, the related issue of reproduction as domestic and specifically gendered labor, and how the division of labor within the work place needs to be addressed as a gendered concern. Clearly, these issues would not be taken up merely as questions concerning production, efficiency, and capital accumulation. As part of a broader feminist discourse, the issue of schooling, work, and leadership would be seen primarily as political and ethical concerns.

In today's global economy, *America 2000* has clearly stated its intention to be the front-runner, with such goals as being first in the world in science and mathematics achievements. Such ambitious goals to improve academic performance are admirable. But what is of concern is the corporate ideology that informs these goals—a marketplace ideology that stresses a more efficient, modernized system that can effectively meet the ideals and needs of a highly stratified economy. "Business interests want an educational policy directed to correcting such competitive deficits, unhampered by commitments to equal opportunity, racial justice, or democratic local control of public institutions."[12] Business will not be concerned with multicultural approaches, homeless youth, children with special needs, parent involvement, or teacher empowerment. In the final analysis, this method of funding will eventually move in a direction, generated by this patriarchal structure, that serves to increase inequality and produce less creative and more competitive and provincially-minded students. Striving to be "number one" in the world is a colonialist sentiment as it is wrong-headed and impractical.

America 2000 also points to state and local funding as a method of supporting this plan. However, presently, over half of the states are reducing education spending with no federal backup to limit any damage.[13] In addition, state funding displays the gross inequities among states, districts within each state, and even schools within each district. Without federal policy to reduce these inequities, the discrepancies between the rich and poor districts will become even more grossly disproportionate. Furthermore, to argue against providing money to public schools at a time when many states across the country are facing major cutbacks and curtailments is morally irresponsible. And finally, to expect to rely on state lotteries to keep schools furnished in construction paper and gym equipment is the ultimate insult to our nation's children.

If only 535 new schools will be funded for the initial program, which represents less than 1% of our nation's schools, what will happen to the other 109,465 schools? The issue of funding is a critical and ruthless omission in *America 2000*. There is little recognition of the unequal distribution of educational services for our nation's children. There is also little recognition of the disparate distribution of resources and opportunities. There is absolutely no recognition that 39.5% of American children under the age of six are poor. There is inadequate recognition of the need for universal daycare facilities and urgent economic programs to alleviate unemployment in urban, suburban, and rural areas.

Our nation's poorest are our children. The statistics are staggering: approximately 40% of children under the age of six are poor, which translates into more than 12.6 million children.[14] However, being poor is not directly related to race—two-thirds of our nation's poor are white.[15] Nor is poverty only confined to urban areas. Less than 9% of our nation's poor live in major inner cities. As Reed and Sautter point out: "Poverty in America knows no racial boundaries, no geographic borders. The only common denominator for the children of poverty is that they are brought up under desperate conditions beyond their control—and, for them, the rhetoric of equal opportunity seems a cruel hoax, an impossible dream."[16]

Approximately 500,000 of these children are homeless nationwide.[17] Some live in public shelters and privately owned shelters, others live with relatives and friends, and still others live on the street, in condemned buildings, in cars and make-shift tent cities. Furthermore, lack of adequate housing translates into poor health care and serious health problems. Of course, this situation did not develop overnight but resulted directly from the priorities created during the Reagan administration. The defense budget soared during the Reagan military build-up, the United States government cut ten billion dollars from programs aimed at protecting poor children and their families.[18] In addition, the Reagan Administration's rhetoric surrounding school reform translated into nothing more than a cover-up for reduced federal expenditures for public education and cutback funding for compensatory programs like Head Start. During the Bush Administration monies were replenished for compensatory programs such as Head Start, but this needs to be placed within a context. A bill was signed on January 21, 1992 to generate an additional 600 million dollars for Head Start Programs. This amount does sound impressive; however, federal funding for additional services will only serve one-third of the children who are in need of assistance. This by no means will adequately prepare all children in America to start school ready to learn. Is ours a nation incapable of offering its children support for decent and healthy lives?

On a more ideological level, the funding policy for *America 2000* reveals a notion of the social good that can only be supported by private interests. In this case, school funding operates in principle to mimic the market. Submitted to market discipline, schools as public institutions, whose purpose and meaning cannot be measured according to the logic of business machines, will not only be underfunded, they will also manifest more radically all of the inequalities that characterize the wider society. Viewed from this perspective, those schools that have the resources, staff, and private support will thrive while those schools that serve the poor and the underclass will be overburdened and hopelessly incapable of providing a basic education to its constituencies. The attack on school funding is in the broader sense symptomatic of the attack on all public institutions that has occurred during the last decade under the Reagan/Bush Administrations.

TESTING AND STANDARDS

Another major component of *America 2000* is the issue of testing and standards. It is noted in this document that the authors had no intention of federalizing the educational system through mandatory national tests and a national curriculum. However, what is proposed are "World

Class Standards" for each of the five core subjects which represent the nation's academic expectations for American children. In addition, somewhere in the midst of all the excitement, the arts, foreign language, and multicultural issues were forgotten. These omitted areas are the very ones which stimulate imaginations and analyze diverse cultures.[19] Moreover, the emphasis on only five subjects that are directly tied to new standards and the projected development of an achievement test can only mean one thing—a standardized curriculum.

It is highlighted in *America 2000* that these tests are "voluntary" and will be used only "to foster good teaching and learning as well as to monitor student progress."[20] However, directly related to "voluntary testing" is the recommendation that colleges will be urged to use tests in the admission process and employers will be encouraged to consider the test scores when hiring potential employees. In addition, federal funds will be provided for only those schools who will adopt national testing. In conclusion, these tests can hardly be considered voluntary!

At a time when major research is presently exposing the discriminating effects standardized testing has on minority and female students and the negative effects it has on both teachers and students,[21] it is disconcerting that *America 2000* is calling for the creation of national standardized tests. Giroux and McLaren address this issue:

> Testing has become a code word for training educational leaders in the language of management, measure and efficiency. Testing has also become the new ideological weapon in developing standardized curricula that ignores cultural diversity, in defining knowledge narrowly in terms of discrete skills and decontextualized bodies of information, and in ruthlessly expunging the language of ethics from the broader purpose of teaching and schooling.[22]

Assessments for students are needed. However, standardized testing has multiple shortcomings that need to be addressed. It is well accepted that test scores are strongly influenced by the social and economic circumstances of students. These are powerful negative forces that discriminate against certain students while privileging others. Howe addresses these constraints by stating that "test results reflect the educational opportunities lost to poverty, racial and cultural discrimination, and lower financial support of some schools."[23] Yet, rather than address the discrimination embedded within them, standardized tests have generated methods for "a kind of sorting and tracking mechanism that promote educational stratification (as to) justify quality on the basis of merit."[24] The political nature of testing and their sorting function is effectively described at length by Linda Darling-Hammond:

> American testing is dominated by norm-reference, multi-choice instruments designed to rank students cheaply and efficiently. These instruments were initially created to make tracking and sorting of students more efficient; they were not designed to support or enhance instruction.[25]

Standardized tests undermine the ability of students to develop their capacities to think critically and engage in analytic discussions. In fact, research shows that multiple choice basic skills tests require students to listen, read, and respond briefly and to question without engaging or initiating anything on their own. In addition, standardized tests require teachers to employ rote-oriented instruction, transforming teachers into clerks and students into machines. Furthermore, it both demoralizes teachers and sabotages presently successful programs by denying funding for those schools that are committed to innovative and alternative methods and procedures for evaluating students' progress and achievement. Instead, standardized tests create binary oppositions between winners and losers.[26]

Lastly, there is the issue of the special incentives for twelfth-graders who excel on these exams. This bonus is a Presidential Citation Award employed to motivate students to learn. Can one really believe that this "personal touch" will create the needed motivation to reduce the drop out rate in urban areas like New York City where the drop out rate for non-white children exceeds 70%?[27] Of course, it will celebrate those who deserve such an award for their achievements; however, it is not an adequate strategy for educational reform because, again, it is based solely on test scores that discriminate on the basis of class, gender, culture, and race. Howe is instructive in identifying what these presidential awards leave out: "A presidential citation award ... does nothing to address the issue of those students who already feel undervalued, neglected, disenfranchised or severely chastened by our schools: the many with low self-esteem, who find themselves repeatedly at risk of failing."[28]

It is necessary to emphasize that assessment is important for both students and teachers by allowing the students to reflect on their work, and providing teachers with not only information about their students' progress but with information for themselves to reflect on the quality of their teaching. However, the challenge at hand is "the task of making standards both meaningful and flexible in ways that make them relevant to all American students."[29] This kind of assessment is situated within a notion of schooling that rejects learning as a form of mastery but, rather, views knowledge as part of a democratic process, linked to empowerment for all teachers and all children.

Some alternative forms of assessment include essay examinations, portfolios, research group activities, and projects requiring experiments, public exhibitions, and oral and written or graphic presentations, to name a few.[30] These assessments include both short term and long term strategies conducted over months and years and gathered informally as well as within examination settings. In addition, this permits teachers to take an active role in shaping and scoring assessments. These strategies do not create winners and losers; rather, their intention is to promote success for all children. Such skills include: developing comprehensive thinking and analytic skills, working cooperatively, teaching respect for multiple talents and creativity (rather than academic skills within five subjects) and fostering the learning of civic responsibility.

Beneath the rhetoric of testing, *America 2000* wields a full fledged attack on issues of difference, specificity, teacher control, and what might be called a pedagogy of place. Testing in this discourse becomes a code word for implementing a national curriculum, a device for consolidating school knowledge into a uniform set of prescriptions about "what every American should know." Of course, there is more at stake here than the issue of testing. On the contrary, the issue of constructing a system of public schooling on the basis of an unproblematic view of culture as a tidy social formation runs the risk of eliminating cultural differences in the name of a common culture, while falsely equating a singular cultural tradition with national identity.[31] Again, testing becomes a key ideological bludgeon in fostering an assault on both cultural differences and the knowledge that they legitimate and produce, and on notions of identity fostered in traditions of difference, dissent, and opposition. Moreover, the emphasis on testing is a political device that invites teachers to de-skill themselves. That is, it eliminates the need for teachers to be cultural archaeologists, who both see and undertake the necessity to explore the various cultural traditions and experiences that give meaning to the diverse student populations that inhabit the nation's public schools. Similarly, it discourages the development of a pedagogy of place, a pedagogy that addresses the specificity of the cultures, histories, resources, and experiences that students bring to the classroom. In this case, the discourse of cultural uniformity goes hand in hand with the practice of teacher de-skilling.

CHOICE

America 2000 presents choice as an important part of educational reform, calling it a concept at the heart of the democratic idea.[32] While this reform agenda only briefly mentions the issue of choice, it has been a much heralded slogan of the Reagan/Bush administrations. In theory, the concept of choice appears to be an important option for educational reform by offering a number of promises. First, it purports to empower parents of all social classes by giving them equal access and sufficient information to make appropriate choices. Second, in theory, choice claims not to discriminate on the grounds of class, race, or gender issues. Third, the less effective schools will shut their doors and will force out poorly-qualified teachers from the profession. However, as the theory of choice begins to translate into concrete situations, many factors surrounding this issue need to be more deeply assessed.

At the core of *America 2000's* statement on choice is the notion that promoting competition between schools will generate the necessary incentives to improve the conditions to educate all children. At issue here is the claim that those schools that are successful in the education market will attract more students, and in doing so will maximize their financial resources. Yet, by analyzing choice more thoroughly, it can be read as a new form of segregation, creating a two-tier system of public and private schools, ultimately favoring economically privileged students.[33] The major problem with the choice approach is that it suffers from two serious weaknesses. Stuart Hall is worth quoting on this issue:

> It assumes, as classic liberalism always has, that the means of exercising choice—money—is evenly distributed. But the very market model on which it is based ensures that this cannot and never will be so. The granting of an equal right which can only be exercised unequally is a form of "negative freedom." . . . The second is that modernity is more individuated but it is also more complex and thus more interdependent. [Education] like transport, health, public amenities and a host of other things, cannot be reduced in the modern world to an individual calculus.[34]

Given the current inequalities that mark the larger society, it is likely that the choice reform will function against financially poor inner-city schools since parents with the time, money, and resources will more than likely send their children to wealthier districts. In this case, poor urban areas will either have no schools at all or will become holding centers for parents "who work long hours, who do not own cars, who do not want their children to undertake long journeys on constantly dwindling public transportation."[35] In this case, the poor will stay in those schools that are already overcrowded and neglected because their parents will be unable to afford the additional cost for special schools or the transportation and services necessary to travel to a better public school system outside of the neighborhood, while the more fortunate will flee. Furthermore, choice would remove funds from schools that are already in desperate need of help. Jonathan Kozol has documented such a case in Massachusetts.

> The wealthiest and most mobile families in low-income districts are driving their children to the nearest wealthy district, in which teachers receive higher pay, classes are smaller and supplies are in abundance. Since public money follows the child, and since only

those who drive or have the funds to hire drivers can exploit this advantage, the poorest districts are losing their most aggressive, affluent and vocal parents, many of their top achieving pupils and the public money that goes with them. Low-to middle-income Gloucester, for example, has already lost about $400,000. High-income Manchester-by-the-Sea, just next door to Gloucester, has gained $600,000.[36]

Furthermore, choice undermines public education which is essential for democracy. Every child deserves a quality public education and funding for that education has important influences on the quality of those schools. However, most children who attend low-income schools receive far less per-pupil expenditures than those students in higher-income schools. In addition, low-income students have less access to well-maintained facilities, small classes, quality equipment and materials, and are provided with less rich and demanding programs.[37] Yet, as documented in Kozol's case, *America 2000* invites both Manchester-by-the-Sea and Gloucester to help themselves. By beginning with such enormous inequities, Bush not only ridicules but conceals the real educational problems that our country needs to confront. Giroux and McLaren address the absences within the concept of choice.

> It is totally indifferent to the social, political, and economic constraints forged in hierarchies and webs of power, domination, and difference that limit large segments of the population from owning even the most basic forms of economic and symbol capital. Competition, mobility, getting access to information, dealing with bureaucracies, providing adequate health and food for one's children are not simply resources every family possess in equal amounts. Without these resources, choices are not so easy since the overwhelming burdens of every day life usually prevent the capacity or possibility for thinking about implementing them.[38]

If the concept of choice were intended to serve all children, then educational reform would offer strategies for using diversity as a strength upon which children could learn about difference from one another, where parents and teachers would have a voice about the design of educational communities. It would also create a framework to learn tolerance, to offer guidelines to promote social, racial, ethnic, and academic diversity and to provide resources to ensure equity.[39] Unfortunately, this approach to choice does none of these things. In fact, the current choice approach to public education accentuates a legacy of choice that is deeply implicated in creating not resolving the problems of race and class that have confronted this country for over a hundred years. It is worth noting that court ordered segregation first appeared in the South during the 1950s in an effort to use public funds for private schools.[40] The present plan is no different. Giroux and McLaren elaborate on this point:

> As a part of an effort to reprivatize public schooling, choice simply becomes a code word in this plan to provide public funding for private schools. But more importantly, it offers middle and upper class parents the opportunity to remove their students from schools that are increasingly becoming more ethnically and racially diverse.[41]

REFRAMING THE SCHOOL REFORM AGENDA

When Bill Clinton took office in 1993, a wave of hope passed overhead. His administration has provided important steps in the progress of social reform in this country. Health care for all citizens has tremendous implications for youth and adults to enjoy healthy and productive lives. This also has a powerful impact on children's motivation and performance in schools.

In March of 1994, the Clinton Administration passed *Goals 2000: Educate America Act*, a version of the *America 2000* reform agenda with numerous modifications. An immediate $105 million was appropriated to launch this reform package.[42] In addition, a number of key provisions have been added. Two additional goals were put forth in *Goals 2000: Educate America Act* which include parental participation, and teacher education and professional development. The National Education Goals Panel has been formally authorized to codify the eight national education goals. Furthermore, all academic areas have been acknowledged, including the arts and foreign language.

A number of new forums have been established. A nineteen member National Education Standards and Improvement Council has been created to develop model national standards and certify standards voluntarily submitted by states. The National Skill Standards Board, made up of a twenty-eight member panel, with representatives from education, labor, and business will make decisions on funding for voluntary skill standards. Furthermore, $400 million has been appropriated for State and Local Systemic Improvement Grants. Additional funds have been secured for Educational Research, Safe Schools grants, Parental Assistance Centers, International Education, and Minority-Focused Civics Education Programs, to name a few. Eliminated from this reform package is the concept of school choice.

Such ambitious goals to systematically improve the quality of schooling and academic performance are admirable. Yet the corporate ideology that informs this legislation is identical to *America 2000*. This is a language that stresses a more efficient, modernized system that can effectively meet the ideals and needs of a highly stratified economy. In this sense, the basic principals have not changed with this new education act. The language of moral, political, and civic responsibility has not been inserted into the discourse of educational reform, and therefore, the defining principles have stayed the same. Ultimately, at the heart of *Goals 2000* is the strategy to attain greater economic competitiveness;[43] however, what must not be overlooked is the funding provided in this reform package.

Clinton's educational reform has acknowledged the need for a federal policy to reduce the grossly disproportionate discrepancies between the rich and poor disctricts. Within this new law there is the recognition of the disparate distribution of resources and opportunities as well as the unequal distribution of educational services for our nation's children. The reform strategy of the "opportunity to learn standards," coupled with federal monies that are needed to address these equities is on the right track. In this case, Clinton has incorporated the principles of social justice to the sphere of economic life.

In spite of this valuable provision to improve schools for many children, the language and prescriptions of *Goals 2000* continues to stress hierarchical relationships, individualism, and bureaucratic rationality. This is evident in the language of standardization. Inherent in the notion of standardized testing is the dubious assumption that this criterion will motivate students to be more successful academically. Comparative testing measures schools, school districts, and national norms, without ever addressing the issues of diversity. Furthermore, the more that standards become the prescription for improving academic performance, the less emphasis and respect is addressed toward cultural difference and tolerance. As noted earlier in this chapter, assessments for students are needed. Unfortunately, we have come to know enumeration as the only authentic criterion of educational performance, whether it's to measure a child's readiness to start school, determining retention, or providing entrance into college.

Another component of standardization is addressed in the "voluntary" content standards. Can schools do what they believe is necessary with federal funding grants if states impose new requirements related to testing and standards of educational success? Although the Clinton Administration does not intend to impose government control, "voluntary" national content standards set into motion an apparatus for establishing a national curriculum by linking performance testing of all students to national content requirements. In this sense, curriculum becomes a carefully specified and structured procedure to tighten the regulation of school knowledge. Control of knowledge and curriculum shifts from children and classroom teachers and into the hands of state and federal government. Mandated new curriculum guidelines set up management processes for schools and districts that provide prescriptions for homogeneous practice. In this case, there is no space for teachers to invent classroom pedagogy based on the lives, experiences, and knowledge that students bring with them into the classroom. Standardized testing reinforces the top to bottom notion of teacher de-skilling, and teacher technicians and students have no choice but to adapt and perform.

Darling-Hammond provides an alternative view of educational reform.

> Rather than seek to make the current system of schooling perform more efficiently by standardizing practice, school reform efforts must focus on building the capacity of schools and teachers to undertake tasks they have never before been called upon to accomplish. Schools and teachers must work to ensure that *all* students learn to think critically, to invent, to produce, and to solve problems. Because this goal requires responding to students' non-standardized needs, it far exceeds what teacher-proof curricula or administrator-proof management processes could ever accomplish.[44]

In this sense, teachers are no longer asked to cover the curriculum in preparation for standardized testing, but rather, take on the role of facilitator to enable students to construct knowledge and make sense of their world. But it is not enough to demand that curriculum be made relevant to students. The goal in how students perceive and interpret new knowledge is not how well they score on tests, but how well students become critical agents. A feminist perspective would elaborate on the issue of educating students to be agents in the broad sense of being able to make choices they can live with. In this sense, knowledge becomes transformative as opposed to accumulated bits of information. Unfortunately, this reform agenda does not teach learners how to govern, but rather, how to be controlled.

DIVERSITY IN AMERICAN SOCIETY

A national plan to reinvent schools that doesn't take into account multicultural issues lacks reality in the present and clouds a vision of the future. Conditions of racism, sexism, poverty, and alienation are embedded in the lives of children that make up many of the classrooms in which teachers work. Female and minority students and children of poverty have been victims of educational and intellectual oppression within both curriculum and theories of schooling far too often. In spite of these concerns, a conservative notion of multiculturalism and schooling still prevails.

What is being enunciated within the dominant language of the conservative position is an undemocratic approach to social authority and a movement to restabilize American life within the parameters of Eurocentrism, racism, and patriarchy.[45] As *Time Magazine* recently put it, "Traditionalists increasingly distinguish between a 'multiracial society', which they would say would be fine and a multicultural society which they deplore."[46] Much of what depicts multiculturalism within the conservative position in schools is developed around the view of pluralism based on the essentialist notion of a "common culture."[47] This version of multiculturalism recognizes that the "common culture" of the United States is made up by diverse racial and ethnic groups, yet requires a universally accepted set of values at its core. This translates into demanding that all Americans, regardless of their histories, cultures, or backgrounds, conform to a dominant ideology. From this perspective there is no attempt to interrogate the notion of power and how dominant groups have more privilege over and silence subordinate groups within this view of multiculturalism. In addition, there is little or no understanding of how the Eurocentric curriculum excludes and marginalizes the voices of women, people of color, poor, and other minority groups; nor does it offer the opportunity to contest positions of power and positions of inequality.

The conservative position of multiculturalism (pluralism) embraces the dominant culture and supports the mighty. This is the working ideology of *America 2000* and *Goals 2000*. Within this position, schools are seen as places that objectively transmit the most important and worthwhile knowledge to those students who are willing and eager to take a piece of the American dream. At the core of *America 2000* and *Goals 2000* social issues are reduced to personal attributes. Here, Horatio Alger lives on as the universal symbol of the successful, white, male, agent of United States history. Nowhere in this document is there stated a relationship among the issues of democracy, schooling, and citizenship. Education for citizenship is an essential task for educational reform. Bellah links the notion of multiculturalism with citizenship:

> The very diversity of American education allows a variety of forms that would link intellect with character and citizenship. For these to flourish we must make changes throughout our institutional life, particularly in our economic and governmental institutions, changes that would show that we understand education less obsessively in terms of "infrastructure for competition" and more as an invaluable resource in the search for the common good.[48]

In opposition to the conservative view of pluralism, the feminist view of multiculturalism defines difference as an important part of the politics of empowerment. It takes seriously questions regarding how the production of knowledge needs to be extended to the voices, histories, and forms of learning that students already posses when they enter the classroom. Rather than demanding a common culture, this position emphasizes a common ground for dialogue.[49] Within this discourse, multiculturalism affirms difference by challenging the totalizing, sexist, and racist views of conservatives. It also argues that the legacies of Western culture have to become the objects of critical analysis. Furthermore, what a critical feminist position on multiculturalism does is locate cultural difference in a realm that includes gender, ethnicity, race, and power. This view of multiculturalism does not privilege difference, nor does it attempt to celebrate or exoticize it, but rather, it places difference within social relations that challenge the hierarchy of power. By placing the politics of difference within the curriculum, it is hoped that students will be given the opportunity to raise questions about how categories of race, class, gender, and ethnicity get shaped within the margins and center of power and engage in problems that construct the different and diverse experiences students face everyday.

MULTICULTURAL EDUCATION—A FEMINIST PEDAGOGY OF DIFFERENCE

A pedagogy that includes a critical approach to a feminist theory and practice of multiculturalism—what I develop in further detail in my final chapter—should emphasize a number of issues. First, it should give students the opportunity to discover their hidden histories and to recover them. This means that the identity of any group cannot be grounded in a notion of history that is unchanging, monolithic, or static. Identities are always subject, as Stuart Hall points out, "to the 'play' of history, culture, and power."[50] Consequently, identities undergo constant transformations. The relationship between history and identity is a complex one and cannot be reduced to unearthing hidden histories that are then mined for positive images. On the contrary, educators need to understand and develop in their pedagogies how identities are produced, how they take up the narratives of the past through the stories and experiences of the present. In this case, multicultural education is not wedded to the process of narrating an authentic history, but to the dynamics of cultural recovery, which involves a rewriting of identity through a retelling of the historical past.[51]

Second, a multicultural feminist theory of schooling must incorporate into its pedagogies a theory and politics of representation. Critical educators need to understand more clearly how social forms and language signify, how they inscribe meaning within relations of power that offer images that represent the identities of others. At the simplest level, this means taking seriously how representations produce meaning, desires, and values through various audio, visual, and print technologies. It means addressing the concept of literacy as a form of cultural politics, one that is attentive to how the incorporation of the everyday is mobilized within the text of mass culture to produce particular relations between the margins and the centers of power. It also means challenging those representations that produce racism, sexism, and colonialism through the legacy of ethnocentric discourses and practices. But more is demanded here than an understanding of the new technologies of representation and how they are used to fix identities within relations of domination and subordination. Critical educators also need to use these technologies as part of a counter-narrative of emancipation in which new visions, spaces, and discourses can be developed that offer students the opportunity for rewriting their own histories within rather than outside of the discourse of critical citizenship and cultural democracy.

Third, a multicultural feminist theory of schooling must refuse the empty pluralism that has often served to contain cultural differences.

Within this discourse, difference is abstracted from the discourse of power and history. Generally naming difference then becomes the first step in policing it so that it can be integrated into the dominant culture. In the name of a common culture, pedagogy then serves to strip cultural differences of their history, uniqueness, and identities. In opposition to this, teachers need a notion of cultural difference that makes power and struggle central to any discourse about multiculturalism. In this case, all students would study their own ethnicities and histories so as to gain some sense of those complex cultural locations that have provided them with a sense of voice, place, and identity. In this way, students could be made more attentive to not simply the struggles that inform their own identities but also to other struggles around culture and voice that often seem to have no relationship to their own lives. I am particularly concerned here about making whiteness visible as an ethnic category, by helping white students understand how their own identities are neither beyond ethnicity, history, privilege, nor struggle. Whiteness makes itself invisible in order to hide the workings of its own power and the ways it secures authority.[52] But at the same time it displaces the foundation for reappropriating its own history and diverse locations. Cultural difference must be taken up as a relational issue and not as one that serves to isolate and mark particular groups. This has important pedagogical implications. For example, Bob Suzuki discovered that in a class he was teaching on multicultural education, many of his white students were ignorant of their own Irish, working class histories. He writes:

> When I asked my students to share what they knew about their ethnic and cultural backgrounds with the rest of the class, students of color—especially African-American students—usually has the most knowledge of their family histories. White ethnic students were generally the least knowledgeable, and after they listened to the long narratives of the students of color, they would be somewhat intimidated and say—sometimes rather forlornly—"I wish I had something to contribute, but I don't know much about my background. In fact, I don't even have a culture." At first, I found such statements astonishing because I hadn't realized the extent to which ethnic experience has been literally obliterated for many

white ethnics. Once I gained that realization, however, I could deal much more effectively with these students.[53]

Suzuki believes that a deeper understanding of their own histories might help students from both dominant and subordinate groups to be more empathetic towards addressing, engaging, and transforming many of the conflicts such groups have had with each other. Pedagogically, Suzuki offers educators the insight that multicultural education should include not only the histories, experiences, and languages of subordinate groups but should include those of white ethnics as well. But, of course, if teachers are to take the issue of cultural differences seriously, then what is at stake here is not merely developing forms of mutual understanding but addressing how such differences can lead to greater forms of cultural democracy.

In the final analysis, multiculturalism informed by the imperatives of a feminist theory is not merely about difference and equity. As a political project, it must address real life issues: massive unemployment of people of color, illiteracy plaguing millions of children and adults, overcrowded and dilapidated schools, youth gangs, homeless children and their parents, violence against minority children, and the refusal to recognize the relationship among inequality, power, and difference in our own "democracy." While a feminist politics of difference attempts to take on these issues, it doesn't automatically lead to significant changes in critical priorities and institutional discourses of power. However, it does offer opportunities for critical discussion to take place allowing for the process to begin.

NOTES

1. Renato Rosaldo, *Culture and Truth: The Remaking of Social Analysis* (Boston: Beacon Press, 1989), p. ix.
2. On the issue of democracy and schooling, see John Dewey, *Democracy and Education* (New York: The Free Press, 1944); Henry A. Giroux, *Schooling and the Struggle for Public Life* (Minneapolis: University of Minnesota Press, 1988).
3. *America 2000: An Education Strategy* (Washington, D. C.: U.S. Department of Education, 1991), p. 19.
4. *America 2000*, Ibid., pp. 36–37.

5. *America 2000*, Ibid., p. 34. See also Joe L. Kincheloc and Shirley R. Steinberg, eds., *Thirteen Questions: Reframing Education's Conversation* (New York: Peter Lang, 1993, 1995).
6. Stephen Ball, *Markets, Morality and Equality in Education* (London: the Tufnell Press, 1990), p. 1.
7. George Kaplan, "Scapegoating the Schools," in Samuel Halperin, ed., *Voices from the Field: 30 Expert Opinions on America 20000, the Bush Administration Strategy to 'Reinvent' America's Schools* (Washington, D. C.: William Grant Foundation, 1991), pp. 11–12.
8. Henry A. Giroux and Peter McLaren, "*America 2000* and the Politics of Erasure: Democracy and Cultural Difference Under Siege," *The International Journal of Educational Reform 1*(2) (April 1992), p. 100.
9. *America 2000*, op. cit., pp. 25–26.
10. Deborah Meier, "Bush and the Schools: A Hard Look," *Dissent* (Summer 1991), p. 329.
11. Stan Karp, "The President's Hidden Curriculum," *Z Magazine* (October 3, 1991), p. 76.
12. Stan Karp, Ibid., p. 76. Also see, Joe L. Kincheloe, *Toil and Trouble* (New York: Peter Lang, 1995).
13. Stan Karp, Ibid., p. 77.
14. Sally Reed and R. Craig Sautter, "Children of Poverty," *Phi Delta Kappan* (June 1990), p. K4.
15. Reed and Sautter, Ibid., p. K4.
16. Reed and Sautter, Ibid., p. K4.
17. Jonathan Kozol, "A Report Card on America's Schools After 20 Years," *The School Administrator* (October 1988).
18. Reed and Sautter, "Children of Poverty," op. cit., p. 8.
19. Harold Howe II, "A Bumpy Ride on Four Trains," *Phi Delta Kappan* (November 1991), p. 198.
20. Harold Howe II, Ibid., p. 197.
21. This issue has been researched extensively by the Cambridge based research group, Fair Testing. For one of their publications, see N. Medina and D. Monty Neill, *Fallout from the Testing Explosion: How 100 Million Standardized Exams Undermine Equity and Excellence in America's Public Schools* (Cambridge: National Center for Fair and Open Testing, 1988); also see James Crouse and Dale Trusheim, *The Case Against the SAT* (Chicago: University of Chicago Press, 1988).
22. Giroux and McLaren, "*America 2000* and the Politics of Erasure," op. cit., p. 14.
23. Harold Howe II, "A Bumpy Ride," op. cit., p. 198.
24. Stan Karp, "President's Hidden Curriculum," op. cit., p. 75.

25. Linda Darling-Hammond, "Measuring Schools is Not the Same as Improving Them," Samuel Halpern, ed., *Voices from the Field*, op. cit., p. 15.
26. See "New York Report: Ban Mass Testing of Young Children," *Fair Test Examiner* 3(4) (Fall 1989), pp. 1, 6.; Medina and Neill, *Fallout from the Testing Explosion*, op. cit.; James Crouse and Dale Trusheim, *The Case Against the SAT* (Chicago, University of Chicago Press, 1988).
27. Jonathan Kozol, "A Report," op. cit.
28. Harold Howe II, op cit., p. 199.
29. Harold Howe, Ibid., p. 198.
30. Linda Darling-Hammond, "Measuring Schools is Not the Same as Improving Them," op. cit., p. 16.
31. This issue is explored in Paul Gilroy, *There ain't no Black in the Union Jack* (Chicago: University of Chicago Press, 1991).
32. *America 2000*, op. cit., p. 5.
33. Giroux and McLaren, "*America 2000* and the Politics of Erasure," op. cit., p. 102.
34. Stuart Hall, "And Not a Shot Fired," *Marxism Today* (December 1991), p. 13.
35. Stephen Ball, *Markets, Morality, and Equality in Education* (London: the Tufnell Press, 1990), pp. 9–10.
36. Jonathan Kozol, "Widening the Gap," *Boston Sunday Globe* (November 3, 1991), p. A20.
37. Jeanne Oakes, "The Many-Sided Dilemmas of Testing," *Voices from the Field*, op. cit. See also, Jonathan Kozol, *Savage Inequalities* (New York: Crown, 1991).
38. Giroux and McLaren, "*America 2000* and the Politics of Erasure," op. cit.
39. Deborah W. Meier, "Choice Can Save Public Education," *The Nation* (March 4, 1991), p. 270.
40. Stan Karp, "President's Hidden Curriculum," op. cit., p. 80.
41. Giroux and McLaren, *America 2000* and the Politics of Erasure," op. cit., p. 102.
42. Mark Pitsch, "Stage Set for Senate Showdown on Goals 2000," *Education Week* (March 30, 1994), p.16.
43. Mark Pitsch and Lynn Schnaiberg, "Senate Amends, Then Nears Vote, On Clinton's Goals 2000 Measure," *Education Week* (Feb. 9, 1994).
44. Linda Darling-Hammond, "Reframing the School Reform Agenda," *Phi Delta Kappan* (June, 1993), p.754.
45. Simon Watney, *Policing Desires: Pornography, Aids, and the Media* (Minneapolis: University of Minnesota Press, 1987).
46. "Beyond the Melting Pot," *Time* (April 9, 1990), p. 28.
47. Diane Ravitch, "Diversity and Democracy: Multicultural Education in America," *American Educator* (Spring 1990), pp. 16–20, 46–48.

48. Robert N. Bellah, Richard Madsen, William M. Sullivan, Ann Swidler, and Steven M. Tipton, *The Good Society* (New York: Knopf, 1991), p. 175.
49. Giroux and McLaren, "*America 2000* and the Politics of Erasure," op. cit.
50. Stuart Hall, "Cultural Identity and Diaspora," Jonathan Rutherford, ed. *Identity, Community, Culture, Difference* (London: Lawrence and Wishart, 1990), p. 225.
51. Stuart Hall, "Cultural Identity and Diaspora," Ibid.
52. Richard Dyer, "White," *Screen* 29(4) (Autumn 1988), pp. 44–64.
53. Bob H. Suzuki, "Unity With Diversity: Easier Said Than Done," *Liberal Education* 77(1) (January/February, 1991), p. 34.

5

A Feminist Pedagogy of Multiculturalism

I believe that elementary schools are important terrains in which feminists and other cultural workers[1] can intervene in developing curricula and classroom relations that eliminate sexist, racist, classist and other oppressive social practices while creating empowering moments toward a vision of a critical democracy that includes all people. In this sense, I am calling for a different approach to educational reform than presented in *Goals 2000*, one that calls for a revision of schooling so as to reflect and embrace a multicultural future. This is a more complex approach to teaching and pedagogy, requiring teachers to redefine this relationship in terms of a mutually appreciated space for living in the world of difference.

In an attempt to include all children, teachers need to acknowledge that their styles of teaching may need to change. This is not to say that teachers are not well meaning or truly committed to quality education for all children. But teachers will need to shift paradigms from "banking education" which reduces learning to the dynamics of transmission and opposition, to the acknowledgment that there are multiple ways of knowing and create a space for constructive confrontation and critical interrogation of that knowledge. In this sense, classrooms need to reflect a democratic setting, one that builds a community of difference that is safe—a zone of equality—which enhances intellectual rigor and intellectual development. Furthermore, curriculum needs to be rooted in the respect for multiculturalism. Curriculum must be made relevant so that it not only strengthens intellectual development, but makes the connection between knowledge and the everyday to expand our capacity to live more fully in the world. In this instance, multicultural curriculum must be integrated and not tacked on the margins. This does not mean simply adding new material to the existing curriculum by offering students bits of knowledge, but rather a revisioning of a curriculum that fosters the relationship between schooling and democracy.

This is a difficult task. It requires all involved, teachers, students, parents, community members, to become active participants in working through fears, misunderstanding, and conflict.[2] In this sense, schools must educate and support all students, which includes all people from racial and ethnic backgrounds, women as well as men, to become active citizens. This is not merely a call for citizens who simply obey the rules but a pedagogy that encourages children to look at the world and make their own decisions, to ask questions, and live with their choices, in a multicultural democracy.[3]

In this chapter I will attempt to unite the most transformative aspects of a critical theory of schooling informed by the imperatives of a feminist politics of difference. It is at this crossroad among a politics of difference, emancipatory feminism, and a critical theory of schooling that a feminist pedagogy of multiculturalism unfolds. Furthermore, I will address a number of questions: What are the central elements for defining a feminist pedagogy? What are the implications these elements have for constructing particular classroom practices between teachers and students? What is the moral vision and social ethics that justifies a particular form of pedagogical practice?

GUIDING PRINCIPLES OF A FEMINIST PEDAGOGY OF MULTICULTURALISM

In this next section I will elaborate on a number of guiding principles of a feminist pedagogy of multiculturalism. In attempting this I will engage in what Jesse Goodman calls an educational language of democratic imagery, "that is, a theoretical language which is informed by and rooted in images of real (or hypothesized) people involved in tangible actions that take place in actual settings."[4] As an elementary and preschool teacher for ten years in a variety of urban and rural settings and more recently, as a university professor, I will draw on my experiences as well as attempt to imagine classroom practices that inform a pedagogy consistent with a vision that fosters democratic principles of justice, equality and liberation. Of course, these images are relevant to only one particular setting, yet they offer the opportunity for educators and cultural workers to analyze how it might be possible to reconceive some of the insights that have emerged from the educational language of democratic imagery into their own pedagogical practices. This is not an attempt to provide recipes for an elementary classroom, or to develop a list of methodologies or models of feminist teaching, nor is its purpose to imitate what is presented. Rather, this is an opportunity to provide detailed illustrations of my theoretical discourse in a way that presents the dialectical relationship between theory and action.

The guiding principles of a feminist pedagogy of multiculturalism should:

1. Engage in students' experience as central to teaching and learning.
2. Offer students the knowledge and skills that allow them to reclaim their voice and their history so as to enable them to name new identities.
3. Provide the knowledge and skills to rewrite the relations between center and margin as part of a struggle for agency, power, and individual and collective memory.
4. Allow the space for students to reconstruct cultural differences and social identities to produce knowledge that is central to democratic principles.
5. Offer a language of critique and possibility.
6. Develop a theory of teachers as engaged intellectuals.

STUDENT EXPERIENCE

A feminist pedagogy of multiculturalism engages rather than dismisses students' experience as a fundamental aspect of teaching and learning. This is an important starting point for both teachers and students. In this sense, pedagogy views knowledge as something to be analyzed and understood by students and informed by their own experiences. Contrary to traditional educational theory, where teachers are the only holders of knowledge, curriculum becomes understood as a living practice. This is a more complex approach to teaching and pedagogy, requiring teachers to redefine this relationship in terms of a mutually appreciated space for empowerment and shared responsibility. Furthermore, this approach requires teachers and students to understand different "cultural codes" in order to accept multiple ways of knowing and living in the world. For example, after having taught in urban areas for a number of years, I found myself teaching in a small Ohio college town, surrounded by farmland. What became immediately apparent to me was not only that my rural farm students did not understand my cultural capital, but that I had no referent by which to understand theirs.[5] I had to devise a number of pedagogical exercises designed not only to allow the students to understand me but also to give me a sense of who they were, what they liked, what they believed in and dreamed about. At the same time, I had to construct a form of teaching that allowed them to take chances with me, to learn how to use and legitimate their own experiences without the fear of being humiliated or punished. I had to negotiate with care and a critical sensitivity both their values and my own. I was convinced that students' cultures had to be accentuated in such a way that students could locate themselves within their own lived experience in a positive way. Let me illustrate this point.

Maggie was one of my third grade students who did poorly in school. She constantly avoided eye contact with me and rarely spoke during class discussions. I found it difficult and frustrating because Maggie had not found a safe space from which she could speak. Then the unexpected happened. One Monday after she had participated in a "tractor pull" at the county fair, Maggie was overflowing with information and excitement which drew the attention of most of the students in the class and gave me the opportunity to allow her to assert a significant story about her culture. I transcribed the story about her trip to the county fair which further developed into a lengthy account of the work she did on her grandfather's farm in preparation for the event. She then had the opportunity to read and discuss her story with the class. Not only did Maggie teach all of us that day, but she became a border-crosser in that she crossed over into a new space, a place where her voice was legitimated and confirmed.[6]

As stressed throughout this book, the classroom is not a neutral environment where knowledge is passed down from teacher to student, but a complex social site, a borderland—a domain of crossing—that offers the possibility for mutual negotiation and translation where both teachers and students bring with them subject positions that are informed by their class, race, gender, and ethnicity. The teacher "meets and speaks with students who carry with them particular stories, ways of relating to one another, dreams, and experiences of oppression or privilege that deeply affects and mark how they view themselves."[7] In this sense, Maggie's story provides a concrete example of how the classroom can become an active public sphere where the personal shifts to the political.[8] We see the connection made between knowledge and the everyday where Maggie could narrate herself and engage in the construction of that knowledge. It is at this juncture that "a feminist pedagogy legitimates personal experiences as an appropriate arena of intellectual inquiry, and insist on a wedding of affect and intellect."[9]

STUDENT VOICE

A feminist pedagogy of multiculturalism affirms student experiences by giving students the opportunity to "come to voice" from their own histories. As bell hooks writes:

> Speaking becomes both a way to engage in active self-transformation and a rite of passage where one moves from being object to being subject. Only as subjects can we speak. As objects, we remain voiceless—our beings defined and interpreted by others.[10]

Questions concerning the historical and cultural place of students that allows them to speak as active subjects is imperative. This perspective informed one of my lessons during my first teaching position in the inner city with Roxbury students in the following way. As a resource room teacher with mainstreamed students in grades one through five, I tried to teach writing by helping students appropriate the sights and sounds of their neighborhood. A few days a week, armed with cameras, we paraded through the neighborhood streets and photographed images.

The assignment I created was to find the alphabet inherent within larger representations of the community. Using the photographs, the students wrote short stories. What happened next was unexpected and exciting. The students became angry with their environment and community when forced to photograph their lived histories. The narration of their own histories were riddled with contradictions and pain. They began questioning existing social and political configurations that were both internally contradictory and physically concrete. The students now wanted to use this opportunity for a conversation for action. Eventually they began to develop topics around their photographs and writings that dealt with such issues as poverty and environmental concerns directly relating to their own neighborhood. For many of the students, this was the first time they had ever written at length on a topic. Letters were sent to the Mayor of Boston as well as to the city newspaper. For many, this was also the first time in which a learning experience such as writing was connected to the specificity of their historical and cultural contexts. In this case, my students were not only learning to write, but also learning how to express their own voice, one that was linked to the experiences and relations fashioned in the sights, images, and signifiers that informed their everyday lives. What provided the space for the students to produce and construct their learning in a way I had not originally imagined, is the notion of a curriculum without constraints, without borders. Of course, the curriculum was still grounded in an act of literacy, but became the act of "reading the word and the world." By learning to read the world critically students are given the opportunity speak out from their own histories and take ownership and control of the direction of their lives as active agents.

It is necessary to point out, however, that when students speak in their own voice, such histories may reveal sexist, racist, classist, homophobic, and antifeminist sentiments. Of course, such sentiments need to be aired both to allow students to speak from the experiences that shape their lives and to make problematic what is often taken on by such students as either common sense or unproblematic. Students voices embody particular notions of gender specific to the language, emotional investments, and communities of meaning that students experience within particular social and cultural formations. These ideologies need to be affirmed as real and important aspects of how students experience and feel ideologies in order for them to be dealt with critically. Such an approach represents part of a broader project which Kathleen Weiler argues is necessary if feminist teachers are to develop classrooms organized around "goals and teaching practices (which) reveal a commitment both to critique and analysis—both of texts and social relations—and to a political commitment to build a more just society."[11] In other words, the feminist classroom provides important sites where the politics of gender construction and difference can be taken up from the perspective of how power inscribes itself in the very act of teaching and learning.

This position, however, should not over-privilege the notion of student voice or refuse its contradictions. That is, a critical feminist pedagogy of multiculturalism does not stop at simply providing the conditions for students to speak about their own experiences. But neither does it overly-privilege voice so as to substitute critical affirmation for a vague and sloppy relativism. The issue here goes beyond acknowledging that students should be allowed to speak from their own experiences; it also suggests that those experiences are historical and social constructions and embody real ideologies and have concrete effects in terms of the interests they represent. In other words, the issue is not to let the rhetoric of voice degenerate into matters of staged difference, or a form of privatized solipsism, one opinion among many, but to interrogate the interests that inform such voices for the actual effects they have on empowering or disempowering classroom communities.

POLITICS OF DIFFERENCE

A feminist pedagogy of multiculturalism provides the knowledge and skills to rewrite the relations between center and margin by exploring the complexity of difference within power relations that enable or silence different students who come out of diverse cultural/literacy backgrounds. First, teachers must understand how relationships are developed between themselves and others and how one's own place is historically and socially constructed. This is imperative if teachers are to be able to understand whose histories are legitimated and whose voices are silenced within the pedagogical relations that structure their classrooms. Only then will they be capable of rewriting the relationship between margin and center by deconstructing dominant ideologies and, therefore, understanding how knowledge both privileges and silences.

Although many educators have noble intentions in setting up cultural activities in the classroom that celebrate gender, race and ethnic issues, they often end up promoting multiculturalism in superficial and, in some instances, colonialist ways. For example, many schools celebrate their ethnically diverse student population by holding international dinners, observing ethnic holidays, or asking students to parade around their school in costumes. These activities do little to solve the problems faced in schools around racist and sexist issues. On the contrary, these activities not only actively construct colonial relations but are implicated in their reproduction and, furthermore, invoke bigotry and exclusion. Not only do these celebrations romanticize and exoticize the other, but view them as fragmented and passive rather than as complex subcultures that are constructed within particular historical and memory-forming narratives that are continually shifting and open to being recovered and reinvented. "Ignoring such influences can lead to the mistaken and conservative view that ethnic subcultures are rooted in the past and are static and unchanging."[12] In this sense, a classroom community must allow for a space of incompleteness for all to grow, change, and survive.

By incorporating a feminist language of difference into pedagogy, students and teachers can understand how identities and subjectivities are constructed in multiple and contradictory ways. Furthermore, by adopting a language of difference, not only is difference acknowledged, but questions can be raised regarding the *kinds* of difference that are engaged. For example, children need to respect and enjoy the hidden histories from which their friends and they come, including children from white ethnic groups. "Many white ethnics, like racial minorities, have also been victims of oppression and discrimination."[13] Therefore, it is necessary to teach about the historical realities and social injustices in American society so that children can better understand the causes of oppression in the hopes that these inequalities can eventually be eliminated. By having some personal relevance to their own lives, students can see some parallels in their experiences and develop mutual understanding and empathy for others, which can serve as a springboard for new spaces and landscapes. The struggle here is to create a classroom community that supports a zone of equality, one that opposes a consolidation of the world, and supports multiplicity where narrations can be taken up critically and collectively. For example, a Social Studies unit developed around Columbus can give a sense of how stories get produced by interpreting this story from a number of different perspectives, such as viewing Columbus as a founder/colonialist/invader. This provides the students the opportunity to develop an understanding of how meanings produce different forms of domination and possibility.[14]

STUDENT IDENTITIES

A feminist pedagogy of multiculturalism allows for students to reconstruct cultural differences and social identities in order to produce knowledge that is central to democratic principles. It is not enough to say that there will be unity with diversity, that students will respect one another; but rather, a feminist pedagogy of multiculturalism needs to allow for the creation of new forms of knowledge by breaking down old boundaries and allowing for new spaces and connections that both legitimate and produce democratic social relations free of sexism, bigotry, and domination. By creating new boundaries/spaces educators can explore both the old and the new knowledge and generate forms of social practices informed by the democratic principles of liberty, justice, and equity.

For example, my first year teaching in Ohio was a challenging one. The school was located in a small town, situated only five miles from the Indiana border. The make up of my classroom was decisively homogeneous and left me feeling quite frustrated at times. One afternoon when filing into the classroom after recess, Tony arrived crying. I immediately thought he was hurt. Tony was one of three African-American children in my class and the kind of student that commanded an unspoken yet genuine respect from his classmates. After taking a few minutes to calm down, he told me that a couple of kids on the playground had insulted him with racist epithets. For the next three hours, all previously prepared lesson plans were put aside, and our class spent that time working together exploring ethnic and racial differences.

When the school day was over and my students were safely on their way home, I joined a number of my colleagues in the teachers' room. I shared with them the racial incident on the playground and the class discussion that took place in the afternoon. I expressed my concerns about racism and asked the group of six teachers how they dealt with racism in their classrooms. The room was silent. Eventually, one person spoke up and her response to my question was that she did not have any issues of racism in her classroom. At that point the rest of the group agreed that they too had no problems. After a few minutes of conversation addressing what I had experienced, one teacher asked how many of *them* did I have in my class.

After reflecting on the afternoon, I realized that not only was I fighting racism on a concrete level but on an institutional level as well. Yet I too had not fully understood and embraced a notion of multiculturalism that provided a space for all students. However, I knew that I had a set of principles and practices as well as a moral investment to justice and equality. In Boston, my classes were diverse and provided a realm for a conversation of difference, injustice, and action. But in Ohio, where the majority of students were white and middle class, that space did not exist *naturally*. Therefore, it was, in effect, my responsibility to create a critical democratic classroom that supported students' construction of identity, and the opportunity to challenge it pedagogically.

Our discussion on racism did not end that afternoon but continued throughout the school year. Within this context, the classroom became a pedagogical site for engaging issues that undermined the ability of students to be democratic citizens. Tony's experience was taken up not merely as an ethical issue but also a pedagogical one.

Teachers must bear in mind that racism, sexism, and elitism in school environments are not always so blatant, but are usually displayed in ways that are often subtle, such as the discussion that took place in the teachers' room as well as within the curriculum. Therefore, it is not enough to stop a class in order to deal with outbursts of racism and sexism, but rather, these issues must be incorporated into the everyday pedagogical classroom practices that promote nonsexist and antiracist relationships that are not only understood but also felt as an affective investment through everyday curriculum work.

Curriculum can be employed as a powerful element of classroom pedagogy that can promote multiculturalism. It is within the curriculum that an approach can be theorized that will enable teachers, parents, boys, girls, and administrators to intervene in the formation of their own subjectivities and to enable and exercise power in the interest of transforming forms of domination and conditions of oppression into emancipatory practices and democratic possibilities.

Many teachers supplement "official knowledge," such as basal readers and district adoption textbooks, with multicultural/multiracial texts that provide positive images and creative characters for both girls and boys. The goal is to provide students with the opportunity to view the world through a multiple, complex, and contradictory lens with the prospect that these books will expand the conception of diversity in the classroom.

While teaching Children's Literature with pre-service elementary school teachers, I became interested in the American Girl Collection which offers books, dolls, and accessories created around five nine-year-old girls, each depicted during different periods in American history.[15] One of the goals of the American Girl Book Collection is to provide young readers with books that feature smart, resourceful girls and show that their lives are worthy of study. With the millions of books sold, I felt that these texts have specific effects and merit further exploration. At first glance, these books promised an exciting opportunity to incorporate multiracial/multiethnic female characters into the curriculum, but when analyzed more critically, I found that the American Girl Series had seized upon the logic of multiculturalism and history to rearticulate politics and difference into the stylized world of aesthetics and consumption. Unfortunately, the American Girl Series merely uses the past as a convenient vehicle to portray five girls' lives in trends and styles reminiscent of inequities that characterize the present. In this instance, the stories fail to connect their audience with the past by providing dominant regimes of representation and therefore, deleting oppositional historical knowledge.

Educators must become attentive to various curriculum forms which produce different narratives of a national, past, present, and future. When history and politics are disguised in the image of nostalgia, innocence, and simplicity, there is more at stake than the danger of simple deception. History in this sense becomes rewritten as a unified chronological record of events devoid of its contradictory, complex and seamy sides.[16]

As educators, we need to be aware of the fact that even though there is more multiethnic literature being published, the quality of the literature for different ethnic groups, white included, may be questionable. Therefore, all curriculum must be read critically. What this means is that much of what is constituted as accepted knowledge must be analyzed for the exclusions, repressions, and privileges that often go unacknowledged in the language of educators in the classroom. This does not mean that children are denied the actual pleasures of literature, but rather, by historicizing culture and problematizing knowledge we provide them the opportunity to understand a notion of diversity and cultural difference represented in the past and present. In this sense, students are given the opportunity to read and understand history in all its complex forms in order to help them problematize the past and begin to see themselves as historical beings who can challenge the present and create a more democratic future. Finally, educators have a responsibility to increase their knowledge of the distant and recent past in an attempt to generate insights into the conditions and multiple identities and ideologies that existed.

LANGUAGE OF CRITIQUE AND POSSIBILITY

A feminist pedagogy of multiculturalism needs a language of critique and possibility. Teachers need to develop a self-conscious attention to the construction and use of language within the critical feminist classroom. In this sense, teachers do not simply retreat into the language of critique but are impelled to create imaginary possibilities for revisioning classroom praxis. In particular, they need to develop a language that both challenges sexist and racist assumptions and calls into question accepted definitions of gender and forms of domination. To ask teachers to be attentive to language does not merely suggest that they be able to identify how sexist and racist interests are embedded in discourse; at stake here is recognizing that language actively constructs reality and as such must be seen as playing a central pedagogical and political role in any theory of identity formation and in the construction of particular narratives and forms of naming. In this case language becomes an object of analysis as part of a wider concern for understanding how the dynamics of knowledge and power function to create a sense of place, difference, and identity for students in the school classroom.

By focusing on language as an active force in the construction of gender identities, both women and men teachers can become more attentive to their pedagogical and political work by first taking note of how their own identities as well as those of their students have been constructed with a language and set of subject positions that are largely patriarchal. As Linda Alcoff points out:

> It is claiming of their identity as women [and men] as a political point of departure that makes it possible to see, for instance, gender biased language that in the absence of that departure point women [and men] often do not even notice.[17]

This is not merely a call for a new language but the need for teachers to critique all discourses and articulate them towards specific sets of questions that will help create new opportunities for developing feminist, antihomophobic, and antiracist pedagogical discourses and practices. It is within the limits of an institutionally sanctioned patriarchal discourse that these spaces are created which need to include not only women but all people as subjects rather than merely the object of knowledge.

It is important to note that without a language of critique, feminist pedagogy could be appropriated into the status quo. Feminists and cultural workers need a language that both challenges and transforms; they also need to self-consciously reflect on and theoretically invigorate their own language from dominant groups who will constantly attempt to subvert, neutralize, and integrate it. As Giroux points out, "it is not the complexity of language which is at issue but the viability of the theoretical framework it constitutes and promotes."[18]

A feminist pedagogy of multiculturalism invites students to challenge the concrete conditions and situations of their daily lives. Questioning power and knowledge become central elements in the development of a critical consciousness. As Freire has shown us, literacy cannot be disconnected from relations of power. Literacy provides an historical, theoretical, and ideological referent for understanding how people negotiate and translate their relationship to everyday life, both in schools and in the wider society. By placing literacy within the realm of viewing social, cultural, political, and economic dimensions of everyday life, students and teachers can understand how literacy functions to either empower or disempower.

In a class on Critical Literacy that I teach with undergraduate teacher educators, we examine three forms of literacy which include functional, cultural and critical. Functional literacy gives us the necessary skills to read and write. Critical and cultural literacy offers an alternative to the dominant discourse that gives a critical reading of how power, ideology, and culture work to disempower groups of people while privileging others. In other words, critical literacy is being self-conscious about how language and other forms of representation, such as print media, music, and electronic media, work to promote images of ourselves and our relationship to others within the elements of daily life and the larger society. In addition, cultural literacy defines the cultural attributes of a race, class, gender, sexual orientation, nationality, and ethnicity. It produces through its languages or representations maps of meaning which determine how people view themselves and their relationship to others.

Classroom texts as well as artifacts of popular culture offer educators an opportunity to challenge the narrow range of identities they project. In the relationship between popular culture and pedagogy, teachers, parents, students and other cultural workers can theorize an approach to intervene in the formation of our own subjectivities and institutional forms of oppression in order to engage in emancipatory practices and democratic possibilities. Within the confines of district curriculum, topics of discussion oriented toward gender issues can be examined. For example, in an elementary classroom, students might analyze and critique the roles of family members on different popular T.V. shows. By observing these shows, teachers and students might generate questions such as: What is the relationship of power between parents and children? How are these relationships used to empower or silence women? Children? What does this suggest about relations of power between men and women? Between adults and children? How do these programs reflect everyday life experiences? Another example of feminist classroom practice is laid out by Michele Gibbs Russell who argues for the inclusion of popular culture in the curriculum in order to highlight and problematize the everyday experiences of sexism. She writes:

> Take the blues. Study it as coded language of resistance. In response to questions from class members about whether feminism has ever had anything to do with Black women, play Ma Rainey singing, "I won't be your dog no more."[19]

This example provides an opportunity to make relationships around the questions of high status/low status knowledge, high culture over popular culture and how this knowledge is gendered. Furthermore, it allows for the deconstruction of the curriculum around relationships of gender/power/knowledge.

Genderizing classroom practice means creating experiences that provide the basis for making gender issues central to how students come to experience themselves in settings that both challenge and reconstruct their own lived experience of patriarchy. It means providing new communities in which gender relations can be experienced and felt anew, relations that offer the opportunity for more progressive social practices and community relations free of hierarchy, oppression, and domination.

TEACHERS AS ENGAGED INTELLECTUALS

A feminist pedagogy of multiculturalism needs to develop a theory of teachers as engaged intellectuals.[20] Teachers must engage in critical reflection and be clear about the politics of their own class and race subjectivities within the student-teacher relations which they produce and mediate. Kathleen Weiler addresses this issue.

> Feminist teachers, if they are to work to create a counter-hegemonic teaching, must be conscious of their own gendered, classed, and raced subjectivities as they confirm or challenge the lived experiences of their students.[21]

Such a recognition of their own subject positions allows educators to recognize the limits underlying their own views. By beginning with their own positions, teachers can then become border crossers in order to understand otherness in its own terms so as to allow them the opportunity to develop spaces for rethinking their experiences in terms that both name and transform relations of oppression and domination and offer ways to overcome it.

The concept of engaged intellectual is central to a feminist theory of literacies and multiculturalism. First, it highlights the importance of teachers recognizing the role that they play in constructing political subjects. That is, as teachers they engage in a pedagogical process that is both political and ideological. Needless to say, while it is important to recognize that education is a political act, it is equally important to develop a position regarding one's own political project and how it informs one view of pedagogy as a practice which always presupposes a vision of the future. Secondly, a feminist notion of engaged intellectual does more than suggest that teachers take up issues that affirm a sense of public vision; it also points to addressing how the specificity of one's own context can be addressed in terms of its strengths and weaknesses as a site of struggle and possibility. In this case, an engaged feminist intellectual is sensitive to the institutional and discursive elements that constitute the specificity of place in which one works. What is suggested here is that our engagements as intellectuals take place within and across sites of difference that must be dealt with in their specificity rather than in terms that are overly abstract or prescriptive. Thirdly, it is imperative that the issue of authority be addressed as both a moral and political question. That is, what are the grounds that enable feminist educators to wield authority or to have their students exercise authority that produce rather than repress democratic processes and relations. Fourthly, the notion of engaged intellectual does not resonate with the image of the isolated intellectual working alone in order to heroically solve the problems she faces. On the contrary, it draws from the feminist emphasis on building alliances, developing new forms of solidarity, and organizing collectively. I want to finish by stressing this point.

Inasmuch as the feminist classroom exists within the structured limits of a social organization that isolates both teachers from each other and the school from the wider community, this does not mean that collective work among teachers and between teachers and members of the wider community cannot take place. More to the point, one of the problems facing the feminist classroom is that teachers are often isolated within their classrooms, removed from the opportunity to make curriculum decisions, and rarely, if ever, are they in a position to shape school policy. This makes it difficult for feminists within the public schools to either wield power or to work collectively so as to change both the curricula and the relations of power that characterize existing school structures. This is not to suggest that feminists cannot work collectively as much as it points to the existing limits under which individual feminists have to work. Individual resistance has to be linked to forms of collective struggle if a feminist pedagogy is to become successful as part of a broader goal aimed at institutional and policy considerations. Put another way, a feminist pedagogy can only become meaningful in the deepest political sense if it links the struggle for feminist justice to working conditions under which all teachers labor. This is not just a struggle over ideology but also over the relations of power in the most material sense. While different schools lend themselves to different forms of struggle, the feminist classroom can be identified, in part, by particular ideological and social practices. Susan Stanford Friedman is instructive on the issue in her description of components of a feminist classroom.

> non-hierarchical classroom; validation and integration of the personal; commitment to changing students' attitudes towards women most particularly women's images of themselves and their potential; recognition that no education is value free and that our field operates out of a feminist paradigm (as opposed to the patriarchal paradigm of most classrooms).[22]

It is within this framework that feminism as a pedagogical practice enlarges human dignity and possibilities.

CONCLUSION

This chapter suggests that feminist considerations have to play a central role in classroom pedagogy. It argues that feminism is a fundamental discourse for developing a broader notion of democratic struggle and social justice. Put bluntly, feminist theory needs to be critically appropriated and understood as a central concern for creating within schools a political community free of injustice and sexism. Also stressed is the assertion that while feminist theory broadens our understanding of how subjectivities are constructed, it must also be taken up as a pedagogical issue. That is, it must address the question of how it is that students come to invest in and appropriate notions of gender difference that infantilize and subjugate both men and women, how are these choices made, how are they internalized, and how do they gain emotional and rational currency in classrooms. These are not merely theoretical and political issues, they are also pedagogical issues. It is in this connection between the political and the pedagogical that feminist theory must be given concrete expression as part of a broader struggle for developing a critical theory of pedagogy and multiculturalism.

NOTES

1. Cultural workers is an important term because it recognizes the mutually supportive character of the various pedagogical roles through which peo-

ple engage social and economic issues in a variety of sites. See Henry A. Giroux, *Border Crossings* (New York: Routledge, 1992).
2. For an excellent source on school/community reform see *Voices From the Inside: A Report on Schooling From Inside the Classroom* (Claremont, CA: Institute for Education in Transformation, 1992). Also see Joe L. Kincheloe, *Teachers As Researchers: Qualitative Paths to Empowerment* (New York: Falmer Press, 1991).
3. Numerous texts on multicultural education include Theresa Perry and James Fraser, eds., *Freedom's Plow* (New York: Routledge, 1993); Henry A. Giroux, *Living Dangerously: Multiculturalism and the Politics of Difference* (New York: Peter Lang Publishing, 1993); Cameron McCarthy, *Race and Curriculum* (London: Falmer Press, 1990); James Banks, *An Introduction to Multicultural Education* (Boston: Allyn and Bacon, 1994); Estela Mara Bensimon (ed.), *Multicultural Teaching and Learning: Strategies for Change in Higher Education* (University Park, PA: National Center on Post-secondary Teaching and Learning Assessment, 1994).
4. Jesse Goodman, *Elementary Schooling for Critical Democracy* (Albany, New York: State University of New York, 1992), p. 173.
5. On the issue of cultural capital, see Pierre Bourdieu and Jean-Claude Passeron, *Reproduction in Education, Society, Culture* (Beverly Hills, CA.: Sage, 1977).
6. On the concept of border crossing, see Henry A. Giroux, *Border Crossing* (New York: Routledge, 1992).
7. Kathleen Weiler, *Women Teaching for Change* (New York: Bergin and Garvey, 1988), p. 143.
8. On the issue of public sphere see Nancy Fraser, "Rethinking the Public Sphere: A Contribution to the Critique of Actually Existing Democracy," in Henry Giroux and Peter McLaren, eds. *Between Borders* (New York: Routledge, 1994).
9. Margo Culley, "Introduction," in Margo Culley and Catherine Portuges, eds. *Gendered Subject: The Dynamics of Feminist Teaching* (New York: Routledge and Kegan Paul, 1985), p. 2.
10. bell hooks, *Talking Back* (Boston: South End Press, 1989), p. 12.
11. Kathleen Weiler, *Women Teaching for Change*, op. cit., p. 133.
12. Bob Suzuki, "Curriculum Transformation for Multicultural Education," *Education and Urban Society* *16*(3) (May 1984), p. 300.
13. Bob Suzuki, Ibid., p. 309.
14. On the issue Columbus and the politics of representation, see Roger Simon, "Forms of Insurgency in the Production of Popular Memories: The Columbus Quincentenary and the Pedagogy of Counter-Commeration," *Cultural Studies* (forthcoming).
15. Jeanne Brady, "Reading the American Dream: The History of the American Girl Collection," *Teaching and Learning Literature* *4*(1) (September/

October 1994), pp. 2–6. See also Shirley R. Steinberg and Joe Kincheloe, eds., *Kinderculture: Exploring Cults of Childhood* (Boulder: Westview Press, 1995).
16. Henry A. Giroux, *Disturbing Pleasures* (New York: Routledge, 1994).
17. Linda Alcoff, "Cultural Feminism Versus Poststructuralism," op. cit., p. 342.
18. Henry A. Giroux, "Schooling as a Form of Cultural Politics," in Henry A. Giroux and Peter McLaren, eds. *Critical Pedagogy, the State, and Cultural Critique* (Albany: State University of New York Press, 1989), p. 133.
19. Michele Gibbs Russell, "Black-Eyed Blues Connections: Teaching Black Women," in Margo Culley and Catherine Portuges, eds., *Gendered Subjects: The Dynamics of Feminist Teaching* (New York: Routledge and Kegan Paul, 1985), p. 161.
20. Henry A. Giroux, *Teachers as Intellectuals* (New York: Bergin and Garvey, 1988).
21. Kathleen Weiler, *Women Teaching for Change*, op. cit., p. 145.
22. Susan Stanford Friedman, "Authority in the Feminist Classroom: Contradiction in Terms," in Margo Culley and Catherine Portuges, eds. *Gendered Subjects*, op. cit., p. 204.

INDEX

Ableism, 51
Age, 51
Agency, 17, 27, 31, 34, 40, 42, 85
   collective, 8
   human, 16
   social, 8
Agents, 34, 73, 88
Alcoff, Linda, 95
American Girl Doll, 93
America 2000, 3, 55, 56, 57, 58, 59, 60, 61, 62, 63, 64, 66, 67, 69, 70, 71, 74
Assessment, 66
Authority, 1, 10, 17, 28, 31, 47, 74, 99
   democratic, 30
   feminist, 31
   teacher, 17, 28, 29, 30

Banking education, 9, 11, 14, 83
   characteristics of, 10
Border crossers, 17, 32, 86, 98
Brazil, 24
Bush Administration, 56, 63, 67
Bush, George, 56, 58, 63

Change
   democratic and emancipatory, 12
Children
   homeless, 78
Choice, 58, 59, 68, 69, 70
Class, 5, 11, 26, 28, 30, 43, 51, 65, 67, 75, 83, 87, 88, 96

Classroom, 89, 95, 97, 93
   elementary, 97
   feminist, 97, 100
   pedagogy, 99
Clinton, Bill, 70, 71, 72
Collective work, 49
Colonialism, 25, 33, 40, 76, 90
Columbus, 91
Common culture, 5, 67, 74, 75, 77
Community
   educational, 69
   participation, 51
   work, 50
Conservative (ism)
   sexist and racist views, 75, 90
Conscientization, 13, 14
Critical consciousness, 14, 96
Critical educators, 27, 29
Critical literacy, 4, 7, 25, 39, 40, 45, 51
Critical pedagogy, 3, 13, 15, 18, 25, 26, 30, 75, 89
   and literacy, 3
   as liberatory learning, 12
   education, 25
Critical theory, 24, 84
   of literacy, 27
   of pedagogy and multiculturalism, 100
   of schooling, 84
Culture, 65, 67, 76
   and codes, 86
   high, 39, 55

Cultural capital, 13, 86
Cultural criticism, 2
Cultural difference, 1, 3, 34, 56, 59, 72, 75, 76, 77, 78, 85, 91, 94
Cultural politics, 4, 7, 12
  of difference, 40, 41
Cultural production, 2, 34, 51
Cultural workers, 12, 24, 32, 46, 83, 85, 96, 97
Curriculum, 16, 60, 72, 73, 75, 83, 84, 85, 88, 93, 94, 97
  national, 63, 66
  school, 16
  standardized, 64
  teacher proof, 16

Darling-Hammond, Linda, 65, 73
Democracy, 1, 5, 52, 55, 58, 74, 84
  critical, 11, 83
  cultural, 3, 4, 6, 78
  multicultural society, 5, 6, 84
Democratic public life, 56
Dialogic methodology, 18
Difference, 3, 4, 26, 29, 30, 41, 44, 45, 66, 69, 75, 78, 89, 95
  community of, 83
  language of, 44, 90
  politics and, 93
Discourse(s), 25, 29, 31, 77, 95
  and culture, 15
  anti-colonial, 31
  colonizing, 12, 46, 48
  communities of, 40
  dominant, 6, 31
  essentialist,
  ethnocentric, 76
  feminist, 39, 61
  feminist Eurocentric, 44
  literacy and difference, 39
  logocentric, 34
  of multiplicity, 46

patriarchal, 23, 24, 95
post-colonial, 31, 34
post-patriarchal, 51
Discrimination, 5, 64, 90
Diversity, 27, 44, 55, 59, 70, 72, 94
  cultural, 64
Dominant culture, 8, 12, 31, 39, 50, 77
Domination, 15, 24, 26, 27, 33, 43, 45, 48, 49, 51, 78, 93, 98

Educators, 28, 46, 49, 55, 76, 85, 91, 94, 98
Education, 1, 63, 69, 70
Educational reform, 3, 56, 57, 58, 60, 63, 65, 67, 69, 70, 73, 74, 83
  Clinton's, 71
Educational theory, 40
  dominant, 11
  traditional, 9, 10, 85
Emancipation, 13
  emancipatory, 30, 97
  self, 14
Empowerment, 11, 12, 17, 86
Equality, 11, 13, 85
Essentialism, 9, 49
  and determinism, 9
  essentialist position, 27, 43, 74
Ethnicity, 5, 42, 51, 75, 87, 96
Eurocentrism, 1, 74
  curriculum, 5, 74
  ric, 34, 43, 76

Feminism, 31, 50
Feminist(s), 23, 26, 27, 28, 29, 47, 48, 50, 60, 83
  anti, 88
  classroom, 89, 95, 97, 99
  critics, 40
  discourse, 61

literature, 41, 51
positions, 75
teachers, 29, 31, 89, 98, 99
theorists, 34, 43
Feminist notion of difference, 27, 40, 58, 84, 90
Feminist pedagogy, 87, 96
 of multiculturalism, 2, 3, 75, 83, 84, 85, 87, 89, 91, 94, 96, 98
Feminist theory, 4, 26, 39, 40, 43, 46, 49, 75, 78, 98, 100
First World, 32
Freire, Paulo, 2, 8-15, 17-19, 23-35, 39, 96
 and politics, 15
 compassion for human beings, 11
 emancipatory educational process, 15
 liberatory pedagogy, 8, 16
 literacy, 2, 27
 notion of authority, 28
 work, 2
Friedman, Susan Stanford, 100

Gender, 4, 5, 11, 28, 30, 41, 44, 50, 51, 59, 65, 67, 75, 87, 95, 96, 97
 and discourses, 4
Giroux, Henry, 17, 26, 32, 33, 44, 59, 64, 69, 96
Goals 2000: Educate America Act, 3, 55-56, 71, 72, 74, 83
 National Education Goals Panel, 70
 National Sills Standard Board, 71
Goodman, Jesse, 84
Gunew, Sneja, 47

Hall, Stuart, 41, 42, 68, 76
Head Start, 63
Hegemony, 9

colonial, 32
cultural, 9
Hierarchical, 98
 relationships, 56
Historical discourse, 8
Homophobia, 50, 88
hooks, bell, 27, 28, 43, 44, 46, 49, 50, 87

Identity, 1, 3, 26, 27, 34, 41, 46, 47, 48, 55, 76, 77, 92, 95
 national identity, 55, 67
 (s), 33, 51, 85, 90, 97
 student, 91
Identity politics, 30
Ideology, 61, 74
Individualism, 59
Intellectuals, 32, 35, 98, 99
 First World, 32
 teachers as, 85, 98
 Third World, 32

Jan Mohamed, Abdul, 26, 32, 33

Knowledge, 16, 17, 18, 29, 30, 31, 33, 39, 40, 45, 64, 72, 73, 83, 84, 85, 87, 91, 94, 95, 97
 official, 93
Kozol, Jonathan, 68, 69

Language, 40
 dominant, 74
 feminist language of difference, 90
 of critique & possibility, 85, 94, 95
Learning, 18
Lesbians, 27, 46
Liberalism, 68
Liberation, 15, 85
 narrative of, 15

Liberation theology, 8
Liberatory
    classrooms, 16, 17
    pedagogy, 27
Literacy, 3, 4, 6, 7, 8, 9, 12, 13, 34, 52, 55, 96
    as cultural politics, 11, 76
    conservative notion of, 55
    critical, 6, 7, 8, 96
    cultural, 6, 7, 96
    emancipatory, 11
    feminist, 41, 44, 49
    functional, 6, 96
    multiple literacies, 47

Macedo, Donaldo, 12
Male supremacist, 50
McLaren, Peter, 24, 26, 27, 33, 45, 59, 64, 69
Meier, Deborah, 60
Memories
    collective, 30, 85
    dangerous, 35
    historical memory, 7
    individual, 85
Min-ha, Trinh T., 41, 43
Minorities
    racial, 30
Modernism, 23, 24
Moharty, Chandra Talpade, 43, 44, 45, 46, 48
Multicultural society, 27, 56
Multicultural education, 55, 75, 76, 77, 78, 83
Multiculturalism, 1, 4, 5, 40, 74, 77, 78, 90, 92, 93, 98
    and literacy, 6, 98
    conservative notion of 40, 74
    emancipatory, 2
    feminist pedagogy of 3, 4, 75, 83, 84, 85, 89, 91, 94, 96, 98

practice of, 75
Multiplicity, 46, 47
    discourse of, 46
Multiracial society, 27

National Education Strategies, 59
National standards, 57, 60
National testing, 58
New Generation of American Schools, 57, 59
New Right, 1

Oppression, 4, 5, 12, 14, 26, 27, 33, 40, 45, 51, 73, 87, 90, 91, 93, 97, 98
Other, 33, 41, 44, 45, 47

Parents, 60, 97
Patriarchal, 95
    binarism
    discourse, 95
    society, 52, 60
    systems, 50
Patriarchy, 1, 74, 97
    patriarchal practices, 30
    patriarchal society, 29
Pedagogical
    classroom practices, 93, 95, 99
    discourse, 95
    models, 26
Pedagogy, 7, 9, 39, 72, 77, 83, 84, 85, 96, 97, 100
    and practices, 24, 26, 84, 100
    Freirean, 30
    liberatory, 17, 18
    transmission, 39
Pedagogy of place, 28, 31, 66, 67
    feminist pedagogy of place, 30
Pedagogy of the oppressed, 14, 24, 27
Pluralism, 74

conservative view, 75
liberal, 40, 45
Politics of difference, 39, 42, 43, 44, 45, 46, 47, 51, 75
   feminist, 40, 58, 78, 84
   feminist/poststructuralist, 40
Politics of identity, 29
Politics of literacy, 39, 57
Politics of location, 32, 42
Politics of representation, 30, 41, 76
Politics of solidarity, 50
Popular culture, 97
Positionality, 29
Postcolonial
   critics, 40
   discourses, 31
   feminist, 44
   ism, 31
   theorists, 26, 34
Postmodern, 31
   feminists, 27
Poststructuralism, 39
Poverty, 1, 62, 64, 73, 88
Power, 1, 5, 7, 9, 11, 12, 13, 14, 15, 16, 29, 32, 34, 40, 44, 45, 46, 48, 49, 50, 51, 74, 75, 76, 85, 89, 97
   discourses of, 78
Privilege, 40, 74
   unlearning, 48
Praxis, 14, 95

Race, 5, 11, 28, 30, 43, 44, 51, 59, 62, 65, 67, 75, 87, 96
Racism, 1, 43, 50, 73, 74, 76, 83, 88, 92, 93, 94
Rainey, Ma, 97
Reading the World, 11, 12, 15, 88
   read and interpret the world, 18
Reagan, Ronald, 62, 63
Reed, Sally, 62

Reproduction, 27
Research and development teams, 57, 59
Russell, Michele Gibbs, 97

Saulter, R. Craig, 62
Schooling, 4, 13, 55, 74, 84
   critical theory of, 84
   discourse of, 11
Schools, 12, 30, 63, 69, 84, 99, 100
   conservative position in, 74
   private, 58, 68, 70
   public, 58, 67, 68, 70, 99
Sexism, 50, 73, 76, 83, 92, 93, 95, 100
Sexual orientation, 11, 28, 41, 43, 51, 96
Shor, Ira, 25
Social justice, 31, 44, 52, 100
Social theory, 34
Social transformation, 11
Spivak, Gayatri, 43, 46, 48
Students, 28, 66, 97
   experience, 85
   identities, 91
Stygall, Gail, 25
Subjectivity, 29
   class and race, 98
   ies, 51, 90, 97
Suzuki, Bob, 77, 78

Teachers, 24, 59, 60, 66, 72, 78, 86, 92, 95, 97, 99
   as intellectuals, 98
   de-skilling, 67, 72
   elementary, 3
Teacher-student relations, 17, 98
Teaching and learning, 17, 86
   styles of, 83
   to the test, 60
Theorists
   counter hegemonic, 34

Theorists *(continued)*
  feminist
  post-colonialist, 47
Testing and standards, 59, 63, 66, 67, 72
  national, 63, 71
  standardized, 64, 65, 72, 73
  voluntary, 64
  "world class", 64
Third World, 24, 32, 49
  women, 43, 46, 48
Tracking, 65

Unity, 27

Values, 1, 33, 58, 74, 86
Voice, 44, 48, 74, 75, 77, 85, 88, 90
  student, 87

Weiler, Kathleen, 26, 27, 28, 29, 30, 31, 89, 98
West, Cornel, 34, 42
Western culture, 5, 75
Whiteness, 77
Women, 30, 61
Women of color, 27, 43, 46
  third world, 43, 48-49
  white, 46
  working class, 43, 48-49